ARCHIVAL
ATLANTA

pw Buffington
"De Buf"

ARCHIVAL ATLANTA

Electric Street Dummies,
The Great Stonehenge Explosion,
Nerve Tonics, and Bovine Laws:

**Forgotten FACTS and Well-Kept SECRETS
from Our City's PAST**

by Perry Buffington and Kim Underwood

PEACHTREE

ATLANTA

For our Moms, who always
wanted us to write books.

And thanks to our Dads, who
thought our Moms had a
good idea.

ℚ
Published by
PEACHTREE PUBLISHERS, LTD.
494 Armour Circle NE
Atlanta, Georgia 30324

Text © 1996 by Perry W. Buffington and Kim Underwood.

Photographs on pages 33, 100, 108, 113, 114, and 132 courtesy of
Kim Underwood.
Photographs on the cover and page 63 courtesy of the National
Archives and the Road to Tara Museum.
Photograph on page 84 courtesy of Glenna Mae Davis.
Photographs on pages 104 and 135 courtesy of the Atlanta
History Center.

Jacket and book design by Terri Fox.

Manufactured in the United States.

10 9 8 7 6 5 4 3 2 1

First edition

Library of Congress Cataloguing-in-Publication Data:

Buffington, Perry W.
        Archival Atlanta : electric street dummies, the great
Stonehenge explosion, nerve tonics, and bovine laws : forgotten
facts and well-kept secrets from our city's past / Perry
Buffington and Kim Underwood. — 1st ed.
            p. cm.
        ISBN 1-56145-105-3
        1. Atlanta (Ga.) —History—Miscellanea. I. Underwood,
Kim. II. Title.
F294.A857B84 1996   95-52208
975.8'231—dc20   CIP

CONTENTS

*Southerners get indignant
when our history is portrayed
improperly.*

—Margaret Mitchell

INTRODUCTION

Not so long ago, my friend Kim Underwood and I were strolling down Peachtree Street en route to a favorite restaurant for lunch. As we sauntered between the Georgian Terrace and the Fox Theatre, we spontaneously started playing our own version of "Atlanta Trivia." We tested each other with questions like:

- Is Underground Atlanta really underground?
  (Depends on your perspective.)
- How did Crawford W. Long invent anesthesia?
  (Fast hands and a colorful past helped.)
- How did Buckhead get its name?
  (This is an easy one.)
- Where is Tara from *Gone With the Wind*?
  (This is a trick question.)
- What were the original names for the city of Atlanta, and how did she get them?
  (Hint: The city had two names before "Atlanta" was adopted...)

Suddenly, Kim's eyes lit up, and she exclaimed. "This is a book!"

What you now hold in your hands is that book, a collection of anecdotes, tales, yarns, and historical narratives gleaned from a variety of sources— books, newspapers, magazines, hearsay, and interviews with those involved in the action. Millions of people have left their mark on Atlanta, and we have tried to delve into those individual stories to bring history alive. Everything is arranged by topic rather than chronology, to make this fun.

So, welcome to a new look at Atlanta's past. It doesn't matter if you're a native, a wanna be, a just-moved, or just-a-visitor; when you finish reading this book, your view of Atlanta will never be the same.

One other little thing: we have attempted to be as historically accurate as possible. We admit that sometimes we have evoked poetic license and added here and there for local color, but we have never strayed far from the facts. We hope you will find the book a great read. If you do, tell everyone. If you don't, well, practice some Southern manners and, as my Aunt Martha used to say, " Shut your mouth up."

P.W.B

1

★ ★ F·R·O·M ★ ★

TIGHT
SQUEEZE

➤ ➤ TO ◄ ◄

HUMBUG
SQUARE

From
Tight Squeeze to
Humbug Square

THE FOUNDING FATHER OF ATLANTA

Approximately fifty miles below Atlanta is the little town of Zebulon, Georgia. In the 1820s, as settlers moved westward from the Atlantic coast, Zebulon was a bustling metroplex on the edge of the frontier. One of Zebulon's premier citizens was a man named Samuel Mitchell.

One night, a stranger named Benjamin Beckman stopped at Mitchell's farm, and Mitchell offered Beckman shelter for the night. Unfortunately, Beckman took ill, and his one-night stay extended for much longer.

During his recuperation, Beckman "took a likin'" to one of Mitchell's horses. He offered his own horse in trade, but Mitchell didn't believe it was a fair swap. During the negotiations, Beckman revealed that in the recent Indian lottery, he had won Land Lot No. 77, valued at forty-one dollars, which was the difference between

the value of the two horses. As the negotiations continued, Beckman threw this parcel of land into the pot. Mitchell eventually agreed to take Beckman's horse and the acquired land lot as an even trade for the steed Beckman fancied.

Beckman happily rode off into the sunset on his new horse. Mitchell suddenly owned a piece of land about fifty miles north in a wilderness region near Fort Peachtree. Little did Mitchell know that owning Land Lot No. 77 would make him the founding father of Atlanta.

Suing
·OLD SAM·

After Mitchell's death, Beckman's family challenged the title of the deed signed by the two men years before. Lengthy litigation transpired, but the Mitchell heirs prevailed. The land stayed in their hands, while the Beckmans received only a $500 payment from the Mitchell clan.

ANY RELATION?

Although people say there is no family relation between Ol' Sam Mitchell and the Mitchell family of Atlanta (including, most notably, Margaret Mitchell, author of Gone With the Wind), others are not so sure. Margaret Mitchell was a seventh-generation Georgian, which places her family's origin at about the same time as the original Mitchells of Pike County.

THE END OF THE LINE

In the early 1800s, a fast and efficient method of transportation emerged: the railroad. Georgia turned away from its canals and water-ways and began to consider new di-rections for its rail lines. The Western and Atlantic Railroad

wanted to expand south to meet up with the Central of Georgia's northbound line from Savannah. After careful consideration, Charles Garnett, chief engineer of the Western and Atlantic Railroad, determined that the end point of his railroad would fall on an almost perfect spot of land, which was quickly named "Ter-minus" to mark the railroad's end. There was only one problem—the state did not own the land the railroad wanted to use.

This perfect spot for the rail line's end fell in Land Lot No. 77. And so the story returns to the old horse trader, Father Sam Mitchell.

Given today's method of doing business, what happened next is almost impossible to believe. A rail-road official approached Sam Mitchell and told him that his wilderness land was vital to the growth of the railroad and to the ultimate common good of the growing populace. After learning of Georgia's plight, Sam Mitchell *donated* Land Lot No. 77 to the state of Georgia in 1842.

"MITCHELLVILLE"?

Not only did Sam Mitchell donate his land in the heart of Terminus, but he also was responsible for the little community's name change. Reeling from Father Sam's generosity, the grateful railroad wanted to rename Terminus "Mitchell-ville." Old Sam demurred and settled for a street named in his honor, and so Mitchell Street was born. He did, however, ask for one additional favor.

Why Atlanta Is · CROOKED ·

Atlanta is different from most other cities in that it is not laid out north and south. Since Atlanta was a railroad town from the start, F. C. Arms, the surveyor, laid out the town parallel to the railroad, running northwest and southeast. So physically, Atlanta is a little crooked.

Sam Mitchell's best friend was a Zebulon surveyor who, it is believed, also did some work in Atlanta. This friend and neighbor was William A. Pryor. Mitchell requested that a street be named for him, too, and Pryor Street was created. These two streets, now both major Atlanta thoroughfares, are a testament to good friends and good will.

"LUMPKINVILLE"?

Terminus, however, still did not have its new name. Mitchell suggested that the city be named for a person who had played a significant role in both the state's and the railroad's history. He suggested that Wilson Lumpkin, who had served his state as governor and head of the railroad, act as the city's namesake.

Lumpkin certainly deserved having a Georgia town named in his honor. Mitchell, known for his generosity more than his creativity, suggested that the town be named "Lumpkinville." Since "Lumpkinville" did not roll off the tongue easily, and the alternatives were equally distasteful (*Lumpkintown? Lumpkinburg? Lumpkin City?*), the powers-that-be turned to the former governor's daughter, Martha, for inspiration,

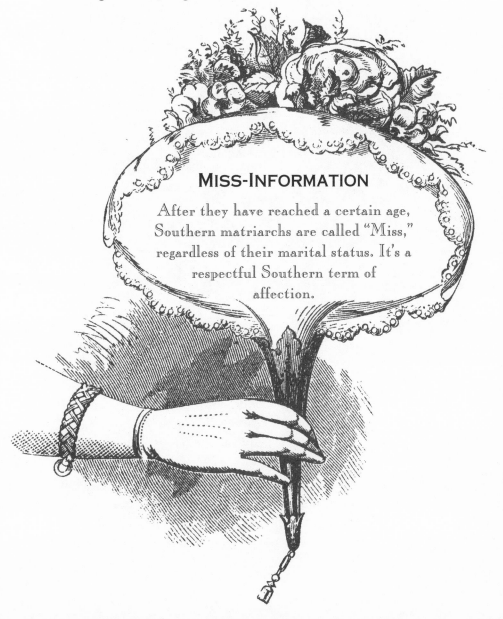

MISS-INFORMATION

After they have reached a certain age, Southern matriarchs are called "Miss," regardless of their marital status. It's a respectful Southern term of affection.

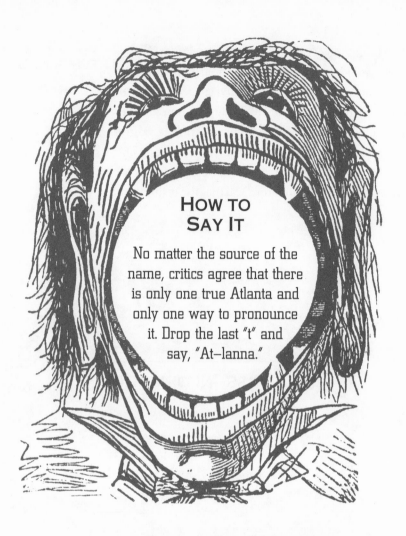

HOW TO SAY IT

No matter the source of the name, critics agree that there is only one true Atlanta and only one way to pronounce it. Drop the last "t" and say, "At–lanna."

and Terminus was named "Marthasville." The name was officially adopted by the General Assembly on December 23, 1843. Miss Martha, interestingly enough, didn't settle down in the town named for her, but instead chose to live in the Athens area.[1]

It seems that from the start, very few residents liked the new name, which they thought much too prosaic to reflect the vitality associated with a railroad hub. A concerted effort to change the name from Marthasville to anything else began immediately.

ATLANTA IS BORN

The Georgia Railroad from the east was about to join with the Western and Atlantic at Marthasville. Richard Peter, superintendent and resident engineer, wrote J. Edgar Thompson, chief engineer of the Georgia Railroad, for any ideas for a new name. Thompson is said to have replied, "Eureka—Atlanta, the terminus of the Western and Atlantic Railroad. Atlantic, masculine; Atlanta, feminine—a coined word—and if you think it will suit, adopt it."[2]

There are some who still believe, just like Miss Martha, that the city was called Atlanta after her middle name, Atalanta. Others believe that it was named for the Greek Goddess, Atalanta. Although its exact origin remains a mystery, the name Atlanta was officially adopted by the General Assembly on December 26, 1845, sixteen years before the War Between the North and the South. The name later was copied by Atlanta, Illinois; Atlanta, Michigan; Atlanta, Missouri; Atlanta, Texas; and the many other "Atlantas" named when soldiers returned home from the Civil War.

In the 1840s and 50s, Atlanta was a "rough and ready" railroad town, and life revolved around the tracks. The

---

The · GATEWAY CITY ·

Atlanta earned the nickname "the Gateway City" because of the railroad. Legend holds that John C. Calhoun, South Carolina statesman and staunch Southern rights supporter, coined this name. He hoped that one day a train would connect Charleston, South Carolina, through the Atlanta gateway to the north.

---

locomotive, which gave the city its origin and life's blood, was honored by a depiction on the great seal

of the city. Streets were laid out parallel to the railroad, and the tracks became an integral part of city life. The city was so active and prosperous that the number of trains passing through effectively sliced the city in half, making it difficult to get from one side of the town to the other. (See chapter 5.)

POPULATION COUNT

With the success of the railroads, the city attracted more and more inhabitants. Atlanta survived the typhoid and smallpox epidemics of 1849 and 1850 relatively unscathed, leaving the city with a hefty population of around 2,500 settlers. An 1850 survey (women and children were not counted in the survey, and some citizens did not respond) breaks down Atlantans by occupation or status:

493 Slaves

70 Carpenters

38 Merchants

18 Free Blacks

10 Druggists

8 Clergymen

8 Lawyers

8 Physicians

3 Printers

3 Tailors

1 Dentist (who also was unfortunate enough to become one of Atlanta's first murder victims)

85 No Occupation (Translated: ruffians, hooligans, gamblers, and vagrants)

The number of Atlanta's residents would triple before the start of the Civil War.

ATLANTA'S NIGHT LIFE

Of the eighty-five citizens listed in the dubious category of having "No Occupation," many were most likely familiar with Atlanta's rougher areas: Murrell's Row, Tight Squeeze, Humbug Square, and the other locations that thrived after dark.

MURREL'S ROW

Named for the notorious Tennessee murderer, John A. Murrell, this section of town was a favorite hangout for thieves, gamblers, cutthroats, and prostitutes. Drunken brawls and cockfights were common and expected here. Before the Civil War, Murrell's Row was the preferred meeting place for those who wanted to fight and concoct schemes. This notorious area north of Decatur Street between Peachtree and Pryor faded away shortly before the Civil War.

HUMBUG SQUARE

While Murrell's Row was known for its cock-fighting and general gaming, popular Humbug Square, perpetually a quagmire of mud, offered more friendly fun. Dancing bears, "freaks," jugglers and musicians, and "drummers," or salespeople, entertained passersby.[3] Most common among the drummers were snake-oil salesmen proffering elixirs, root doctors prescribing fascinating pseudo-medical treatments, and medicine men claiming to have traveled and studied with the Indians.

All the cures were over the counter. Where else could customers get their livers rejuvenated and their fortunes told simultaneously? This area existed just below the train station. A visit to modern-day Underground Atlanta will put you right in the middle of Humbug Square.

BUCKHEAD

In the 1840s and 50s, Buckhead was known as "Irbyville," named after old Henry Irby's Tavern and Inn. This "neighborhood" was little more than a clapboard tavern on the side of the road, off the beaten path from the active railroad yards of downtown Atlanta.

One day, according to folklore, tavern owner Irby adorned his front porch with the head of a large deer shot near the spring in his backyard. As a result, residents adopted the more strikingly descriptive name "Buckhead."

Henry Irby's tavern sat where today's Peachtree Street and Roswell Road meet. The only remaining relic of Henry Irby's era is an old oak tree one block west of Peachtree. Rumor has it that this age-old tree witnessed one of the Irbys

THE FIRST PARTY

The first recorded social event in Atlanta was held in 1850 when Mrs. Mulligan held a ball to celebrate the laying of a real floor (that is, wood over her packed dirt floor) in her cabin.

burying a stash of Confederate gold where Buckhead Plaza now stands. The gold, however, has never been found.

TIGHT SQUEEZE

While Irby's tavern was well known and a popular meeting place, its location was less than ideal in the mid-1800s. The route to Buckhead (especially after the Civil War, when the suburbs of Atlanta became infested with war-displaced thieves and hooligans) required passage through "Tight Squeeze." Composed of a cluster of houses, a wagon yard, a blacksmith shop, and several small stores, Tight Squeeze was notorious as a hangout for those interested in illegal gain. Tight Squeeze began at the intersection of present-day Peachtree and 10th Streets and extended north to the outskirts of Buckhead.

The Farmer Plaster
· AMBUSH ·

One Buckhead farmer found out about the dangers of Tight Squeeze the hard way. As Farmer Plaster headed home to Buckhead after selling his cotton down by the Atlanta rail yards, he was singled out as an easy mark by the Tight Squeeze locals. The thieves ambushed Farmer Plaster and demanded all his money. While Farmer Plaster may have laughed all the way to the bank where he had deposited his profits before returning home, his grieving widow cried all the way back to claim the cash. The Tight Squeeze thieves had killed Plaster for fifteen cents.

TWO PEACHTREE STREETS

Head north on Peachtree Street from downtown, blink, and you'll find yourself on West Peachtree—but don't worry, you're still heading north!

In early Atlanta, the dirt Peachtree Road was a short but straight byway. Rains, along with wear and tear from farmers' wagons, caused a deep hollow in the roadway. When it was muddy, even the best team of horses could not pull a wagon through. Farmers and others driving into town soon took the high road to the east, bypassing the mud and creating yet another Peachtree. After a time of confusion, it became necessary to give the roads separate names.

Welcome to Peachtree Street and West Peachtree. There are, however, no such solid explanations for Peachtree Road, Peachtree Place, Peachtree Manor, and the hundreds of other Peachtree Streets on the Atlanta map.

STATE SQUARE

One of the most emotionally charged scenes in *Gone With the Wind* is the panoramic view of Scarlett O'Hara walking among the thousands of Atlanta's dying, sick, and wounded lying outside the train terminal. This depressing scene is actually a realistic representation of the numbers of injured associated with the Battle of Atlanta.

These wounded men, many waiting to be transported to hospitals outside the city, were placed in antebellum Atlanta's favorite breathing spot. This tree-lined park, called "State Square," sat in the heart of town and was bounded by Pryor, Decatur, and Central Streets, and the Western and Atlantic Railroad. (This was the land deeded to Atlanta by Sam Mitchell.)

When the hospitals could no longer hold the numbers of wounded soldiers flowing into the city, State Square was converted into an open-air medical facility. Men butchered and maimed by artillery were transported there to await their turns on the surgeon's table. Piles of dismembered arms and legs paid silent testimony to the fates of many soldiers.

Sherman destroyed State Square, and it has never been restored. A visit to Underground Atlanta places visitors on this hallowed ground.

CAPITAL IDEA

In only the third decade after the city was born, Atlanta sought the position of the capital of Georgia. When the state's constitutional convention met in Atlanta in early 1886, the city made an offer Georgia couldn't refuse: move the capital from Milledgeville, and Atlanta would put up the legislature free-of-charge for ten years.

On December 5, 1877, Georgia voters approved of the permanent

Atlanta-tude

"If Atlanta could suck as hard as it could blow, it would be a seaport," a resentful Savannah citizen remarked about Atlanta's boom time.

relocation by a nearly two-to-one margin. Early the next year, the legislature moved into the Kimball Opera House, which served as its home until a new building could be constructed.

Twelve years later, on July 4, 1889, the legislature convened in its new quarters, the present day Georgia State Capitol. The building exterior was constructed with Indiana limestone; Georgia marble was available, but was deemed too expensive. One small section of Georgia marble can be found at the capitol's cornerstone, and local marble later refurbished the capitol walls, steps, and floors. In 1958, the building's tin-alloy dome received a coating of forty-three ounces of Dahlonega gold.

Living in
· THE DOME ·

In the early days, the Georgia State Capitol actually had residents. Near the turn of the century, the assistant adjutant general and his family set up housekeeping in the top of the dome. The occupants had an excellent view in all directions of the growing city.

2

★ ★ T·H·E ★ ★

GREAT
UNPLEASANTNESS

·2·

The Great Unpleasantness

Georgia seceded from the United States on January 19, 1861, at two o'clock in the afternoon. The vote to do so was 208 to 89. Atlanta went with Georgia willingly into the Civil War.

THE GREAT TRAIN ROBBERY

Long before the Union army invaded Atlanta, an event clearly foreshadowed the important role Atlanta's railroad would play in the Civil War. It all started when a Yankee spy made his way to Atlanta with

The Civil War goes by many names, especially in the South:

"The Great Unpleasantness"
"The War Against Northern Aggression"
"The War Between the North and the South"
"The War for Southern Independence"
"The Civil War"
"The War Between The States"
"The War"

plans to spirit away a locomotive and take it behind enemy lines.

In April 1862, the North was planning to attack Chattanooga, Tennessee. To help guarantee a Federal success, Union spy James J. Andrews proposed sneaking into Atlanta, capturing a train, and engineering it to Chattanooga. Along the route he planned to burn bridges, cut telegraph wires, and twist the rails behind the escaping train. He thought that destroying this line would stop Southern troops from coming to the aid of Chattanooga. The Union army happily agreed with his ambitious plan.

Posing as a peddler smuggling quinine for malaria, Andrews made his way south with twenty-four men, arriving in Atlanta on April 12, 1862. The group boarded the train known as "The General" as it pulled out of Atlanta around 4:00 A.M. When the train stopped at Big Shanty so the engineers and passengers could have breakfast, Andrews and his men saw their chance and stole the locomotive with only three of its cars attached.

Captain William A. Fuller, the conductor of "The General," saw Andrews steal the train and took out after him. When Andrews had to stop for additional wood for power, he bluffed his way out of questions about the few cars by claiming he was a Confederate officer rushing gunpowder to Chattanooga. The lie worked, and "The General" was allowed to pass.

But Andrews's good luck soon faded. "The General" was delayed for over an hour when it had to pull over and allow a series of larger trains to pass, and soon the renegade group heard the whistle of Conductor Fuller's train in close pursuit. The Yankee spies jumped from the train to escape when capture seemed imminent, but all were quickly caught.

The spies were brought to Atlanta to meet their punishment. On June 7, 1862, seven days before Andrews's scheduled wedding, he and seven of his men were hanged in Atlanta. G. A. Hornady, a Confederate

THE HERO'S MEDAL

What about the hero of the day, Captain Fuller, the man who caught Andrews? His courage, zeal, and intelligence were praised by all. As you might expect, he was awarded a gold medal. Unfortunately, the medal was never cast.

private, said that Andrews spoke little as he was taken into the woods, but did reveal that his reward for successfully stealing "The General" would have been $10,000 and the right to convey cotton through the battle lines. Hornady also reported that Andrews, a tall and handsome fellow, was well aware of the price he would pay for his traitorous actions. He went to his hanging calmly and courageously, as a soldier should. The hanging did not proceed smoothly, however; Andrews was very tall, and when the trap was sprung, his feet reached the ground. A quick-thinking soldier had to grab a spade and shovel dirt aside so the body could drop and hang free, allowing a quicker and less-painful death.

Another seven men of Andrews's spy ring were hanged some days later. Reports claimed that these men died poorly, with fear and crying. Apparently the scene was made doubly difficult by the fact that two of the condemned men were so overweight that they caused their ropes to break and had to be hanged twice.

The remainder of Andrews's men were sent to Confederate prison.

The site of the hangings is a relatively prominent point in modern-day Atlanta. Andrews and his men were hanged near the corner of Peachtree and Ponce de Leon. Back then, this spot was a wooded area on the fringe of Atlanta. Today this corner is the home of the Fox Theatre and the Georgian Terrace.

ATLANTA: KEY TO THE CONFEDERACY

Atlanta supported Confederate war efforts economically from the very beginning, manufacturing all manner of war materials. Although a working industrial center, Atlanta held on to its civilities until the last moment. Three newspapers, the *Daily Intelligencer,*

Creative
· COFFEE ·

Life did not continue normally in all ways,
however. The blockade by the Union army
off the coast of Georgia kept luxuries away
from the citizenry. Coffee was especially
missed, and entrepreneurial types quickly
developed substitutes and marketed them
at exorbitant black-market prices. One
such offering consisted of a mixture of
roasted cereals, sawdust, and just a hint of
coffee beans. Another recipe for mock
coffee called for sound ripe acorns,
washed while in the shell, dried, and then
parched until they cracked open. The shell
was removed, and the inside nut roasted
with a little bacon fat.

the *Atlanta Register,* and the *Southern
Confederacy* reported not only the day's war activities
but also the evening's social events. Religious services
and theatrical performances didn't stop until the Yankees were in the city.

Except for occasional inconveniences and short-
ages, Atlanta had been spared for most of the war; the
majority of the fighting occurred hundreds of miles
away. However, once the tide turned, it was obvious
that Atlanta would be punished for its support of the
Confederacy. In June, 1864, Atlanta was home to the
largest train terminal, was the chief manufacturer of
gunpowder for the Confederacy, and served as the
bread basket of the South. Sherman had to have Atlanta to defeat the Confederacy, and he decided to isolate the city by destroying each railroad that supported

Atlanta. Just as the railroads had prompted the creation of Atlanta, the railroads now converging from all points of the compass would precipitate Atlanta's fiery demise.

THE BATTLE OF ATLANTA

Although their casual attitudes at the time did not reflect any knowledge of approaching conflict, Atlantans did have fair warning of the impending battle. On April 26, 1864, the *Daily Intelligencer* called attention to the "possible"—not yet believed to be inevitable—assault of Atlanta by the Union army. By May 9, 1864, the possible had turned to probable, and notices were published conscripting all males between the ages of sixteen and sixty in service of the Confederate states. On May 17, 1864, a local militia was in place and the first inspection of troops finished.

Mayor James M. Calhoun issued the following proclamation on May 23, 1864:

In view of the dangers which threaten us, and in pursuance of a call made by General Wright and General Wayne, I require all male citizens of Atlanta, capable of bearing arms, without regard to occupation, who are not in the Confederate or State service, to report by 12 M., on Thursday, the 26th. . . . to O. H. Jones, marshal of the city, to be organized into companies and armed, and to report to General Wright when organized. And all male citizens who are not willing to defend their home and families are requested to leave the city at their earliest convenience, as their presence will only embarrass the authorities and tends to the demoralization of others.[1]

Even after such a sobering order, Atlantans did not accept the inevitability of an attack on Atlanta. They were convinced the local militia would protect them. But on May 27, 1864, residents heard the thunder of artillery for the first time; the war was on the way.

The First Casualty of
· THE BATTLE OF ATLANTA ·

On July 20, 1864, Atlanta was baptized by fire when three shells struck the city. Er Lawshe, the local jeweler, reported crossing Ivy at Ellis Street (just northeast of Five Points) shortly before noon on the ninety-degree, humid summer day. He noticed a father, mother, and young daughter walking by Rice's, the lumber dealer's home. He then heard the sounds of whirring, rattling, and "whoosh!" above his head, followed immediately by a loud explosion that stunned and deafened him. When the cloud of dust cleared, all Lawshe could see was the little child face down in the middle of the intersection. She had been hit by the first shell to strike the city. This unfortunate little girl became the first casualty on the first day of the Battle of Atlanta.

FORTY DAYS AND FORTY NIGHTS

The Battle of Atlanta truly commenced on July 22, 1864. Battle lines stretched from the current Carter Center southward along Moreland Avenue toward Interstate 20.

Common feelings and ways of life in Civil War Atlanta—especially during the Battle of Atlanta—were accurately depicted in ten-year-old Carrie Berry's diary. As she put it,

We could not sleep because we were afraid the soldiers might set fire to our house. They behaved very badly, I thought, going round setting people's houses on fire. Wish I could go to school. We are having all hallowdays [sic]. *I wirk* [sic] *at home and sleep if mosquitoes don't bite too much. Soldiers pace back and forth but orderly. We are all in so much trouble. Mamma is so worried. Papa does not know where to go. We had stewed*

chicken. It is a dark, rainy day. The last train has left. We are efbliged [sic] *to stay now.*[2]

By the end of the first day of battle, Confederate General John Bell Hood had achieved some limited success. Over 3,000 Union soldiers, including commanding General McPherson, had been killed. But the Confederates had suffered even greater losses, with over 6,000 dead.

Carefully working his way around the four points of the compass as he had planned, Sherman seized each railroad system; the final struggle of the Battle of Atlanta took place on August 31, 1864. Ten Confederate and eleven Federal batteries took part in the engagement.

General J. B Hood

Over the course of this final battle, great volumes of sulfurous smoke blanketed the town. The sun glowed red through the bronze-colored cloud. On September 1, 1864, Hood's soldiers set fire to the ordinance stores, marching sorrowfully out of town to the musical strains of "Lorena."

The next day, Mayor Calhoun rode out under a white flag and personally surrendered to General Sherman. That same day, Sherman wired Lincoln, "Atlanta is ours and fairly won." Four days later he issued the following order:

> The City of Atlanta being exclusively required for warlike purposes, will be at once vacated by all except the armies of the United States and such civilians as may be retained.[3]

Heeding Sherman's demand, 446 families (860 children and 705 adults) went south. (No records were kept of anyone who may have gone north.) Atlanta had fought valiantly and lost. It was the beginning of the end of the Civil War.

HYPOCHONDRIACS WELCOME

The Federals did have compassion for some of those who remained in the city. The best known physician in Atlanta during the siege was Dr. Noel D'Alvigny, who is credited with saving the medical college from destruction.

D'Alvigny feared the Union soldiers would destroy the college, which served as a hospital during the Battle of Atlanta.

Granny Mason's · MATTRESS ·

Although he was a resourceful wit on his own, Dr. D'Alvigny may have modeled his deception on a similar ruse by Granny Mason. According to family lore, Granny reacted quickly when she saw Sherman's army heading her way. She stuffed the family's valuables under an upstairs mattress, donned her bedclothes, and jumped into bed. Suddenly she became very ill, or so her moaning suggested. When the soldiers looked in, they saw a sick old woman and left. Needless to say, Granny quickly recovered her health—and her wealth.

The wounded had been evacuated when defeat loomed inevitable, and D'Alvigny worried that the hospital might look too empty and be demolished by the invading troops without a second thought. To prevent this disaster, Dr. D'Alvigny filled every available bed with able-bodied men, who, under D'Alvigny's orders, were bandaged up and told to act sick. When the Northern soldiers came through, the pretenders moaned, groaned, and beseeched the Federals not to move them. The Yankees showed compassion, leaving the medical college and hospital standing.

FLAME RESISTANT

The home of Lemuel Pratt Grant, one of Atlanta's civil leaders who had played an important role in the growth of Atlanta's railroads, also luckily escaped the flames. Although born a Yankee (originally from Maine), L. P. Grant became a colonel in the Confederate army and is given credit for designing the fortifications that circled Atlanta during the Civil War. The L. P. Grant house served as a hospital during the war, and was one of only two antebellum homes left in the city after the burning of Atlanta. (Sherman supposedly ordered his soldiers to spare the homes of Masons; Sherman and U. S. Grant were both members.) L. P. Grant's family and friends reportedly stood on the porch to watch Atlanta burn before going back inside for lunch. After the war, Grant donated to Atlanta most of the 131 acres which would later become Grant Park. (See chapter 9.)

The L. P. Grant House was severely damaged by two different fires long after the danger of the Civil War was over; the roof is entirely gone. Only two of the home's original three stories can be restored; the walls will not withstand the weight of a third story. The Grant House is located just west of Grant Park on St. Paul Avenue.

GOOD RIDDANCE

Capturing Atlanta was not enough to punish the economic linchpin of the South. The city was set afire when Sherman's troops left the city and began the March to the Sea. Over 4,500 buildings were destroyed, including every building devoted to education. Only a handful of buildings were spared. (See chapter 3.)

On November 15, 1864, Sherman wrote of leaving Atlanta by Decatur Road: "Behind us lay Atlanta, smoldering and in ruins, the black smoke rising high in the air, and hanging like a pall over the ruined city." He also wrote, as though to clear his conscience, "I peremptorily required that all citizens and families should go away."[4] When he departed from Atlanta, the infamous March to the Sea was underway; this march ended when Sherman gave the defeated city of Savannah to President Lincoln as a Christmas present. Within a matter of months, the war would be over.

STARTING OVER

On December 2, 1864, approximately two weeks after Sherman left Atlanta in flames to set out on his March to the Sea, Confederates returned to the city. Mayor Calhoun also returned to begin the resurrection process. He found only $1.64 left in the city treasury.

It was the worst of times, and it would be a while before it was the best of times for Atlanta. The city was in ashes. Stores, banks, factories, railroads, educational buildings, hotels, and churches were all destroyed by the fire. Confederate money was plentiful but worthless, while Union money was unavailable. There were no products to buy except on the black market. Sherman had destroyed the land between Atlanta and Savannah, so the agricultural growing season was virtually nonexistent.

The battles continued, but the South had already lost the war. Confederate General Robert E. Lee surrendered to Union General Ulysses S. Grant on April 9, 1865. Although the South was technically vanquished, both sides lost. Less than one week after the surrender, President Abraham Lincoln was assassinated.

JOHN WILKES BOOTH IN ATLANTA?

After John Wilkes Booth assassinated Abraham Lincoln, rumors were rampant that Booth had escaped capture. Cover-ups and conspiracies surrounding Lincoln's death were the hottest topics of conversation. Who actually killed Lincoln? How badly was Booth hurt when he jumped from Lincoln's balcony at Ford's Theatre? Who was the Dr. Mudd who set Booth's broken leg, and was he

THE SHRINKING FARMS

•

In just a few years, the average farm declined in size from one hundred acres before the war to thirty acres after the war.

•

part of the conspiracy? Was there a password which had allowed Booth to pass through Union lines into the friendlier South? Many people believed that John Wilkes Booth was alive and well; after all, he was an actor and a master of disguise.

Booth was considered a dashing fellow: tall and handsome, with raven-black hair, dark eyes, stylish clothing, and gentlemanly mannerisms. Before the assassination, he had been the swain of choice for many a theater-going female. After Lincoln's death, Booth's name and picture were recognized in almost every household in the United States. Then a rush of excited apprehension struck Atlanta: John Wilkes Booth was sighted in the city.

A man with Booth's coal-black eyes, dramatic ways, and raven hair moved to Atlanta. He did not look exactly like the pictures of Booth, but the populace quickly explained the discrepancies. He wore his hair long to hide a scar on the back of his neck, a tell-tale sign that he had been hurt in his escape from Ford's Theatre and was covering up his injury. There was another characteristic that identified the newcomer as the real John Wilkes Booth without a doubt—the newcomer had a lame leg!

Then the frenzied talk subsided. The Atlanta Booth look-a-like turned out to be the Reverend J. G. Armstrong, the new pastor of The Cathedral of St. Philip Episcopal. Armstrong had come to Atlanta from Richmond, where he was also often mistaken for Booth. Despite the final explanation, the curiosity of the people filled the seats and the coffers of St. Philip's for many Sundays. The Cathedral of St. Philip stands at 2744 Peachtree Road.

THE ETERNAL FLAME

Just after the Civil War's conclusion, a war-scarred lamppost was moved from its original position at the northeast corner of Alabama and Whitehall Streets to City Hall to serve as a reminder of the human and economic tolls of the Battle of Atlanta.

In 1880, the city moved the lamp back to its original spot. In 1919 the United Daughters of the Confederacy commemorated the lamp as the "Eternal Flame of the Confederacy" and dedicated it to Confederate veteran General A. J. West. At the time of the premiere of *Gone With the Wind*, the lamp was rededicated, and The Atlanta Gas Light Company converted the lamp to natural gas, donating the gas for the flame free of charge.

There the Eternal Flame stayed for more than forty years until the rapid-transit railroad, MARTA (Metro Atlanta Rapid Transit Authority), began construction. The Eternal Flame was removed to make way for the new railroad. Atlanta Gas placed the lamp in storage until the MARTA construction was complete. The lamp was reinstalled and relit on September 9, 1982.

One of Atlanta's twin Eternal Flames, this one stands outside McElreath Hall at the Atlanta History Center.

The Eternal Light of the Confederacy has a twin in Atlanta. This illumination is located outside McElreath Hall at the Atlanta History Center. These two lamps were the only gas lampposts left over when Atlanta converted to electric power. The twin post originally burned in front of the Bell House, an exclusive boarding house for men.

3
HEROES
➤ ➤ AND ◄ ◄
VILLAINS

·3·

Heroes and Villains

THE DOCTOR WILL SEE YOU NOW

Technically, Crawford W. Long is not from Atlanta. In fact, Long was born in Jefferson, Georgia, and spent only one full year in Atlanta before settling in Athens. Despite these facts, Atlanta has adopted him as a favorite son and has memorialized him in recognition of his influence on modern medicine.

Two circumstances led Dr. Long to the discovery that helped to reshape medicine. The first concerned a surgeon's swiftness.

In the early 1800s, surgery was dreaded and postponed as long as possible because there was no way to deaden pain other than to dull it with whiskey. To minimize their patients' suffering, surgeons had to perform operations as quickly as possible. Despite the doctors' efforts, however, many patients died, fully conscious, on the surgeon's table. Long was supposedly one of the swiftest surgeons of his day, but he never was able to accustom himself to

the inevitable suffering and screams of those strapped to his operating table.

In the fall of 1841, some friends asked Long to contribute "laughing gas" for a party that evening. Long had none and suggested sulfuric ether instead. He warned his friends to use it cautiously, recounting the story of a friend in Pennsylvania who had completely lost consciousness from an overdose. After inhaling the sulfuric ether, his friend had fallen, broken a glass, and cut his arm badly, but he did not feel the pain from the wound until he saw blood. It was this tale that served as the second impetus to Dr. Long's thinking about painless surgery.

On March 30, 1842, James Venable came to Long's office to have one of two tumors removed from the back of his neck. Long suggested Venable try sulfuric ether as a possible way to ease the pain. Either that, or Edmund Rawls would serve as the surgery witness and assistant—it took at least one person to hold the patient on the table while the surgeon plied his trade. Venable agreed to Long's first suggestion and tried the ether.

> ## ETHER FROLICS
>
> Long had experimented with the recreational drugs of the day while in medical school. Ammonium nitrate (laughing gas, which is still used by dentists) and sulfuric ether were all the rage, and available over the counter.

Not knowing the exact effects of ether, Long operated quicker than ever before. He operated so rapidly, in fact, that his patient said, "Go ahead, Doctor, and get it over!" not realizing the surgery was completed. The cost of Venable's surgery was two dollars, with an extra twenty-five cents for the ether.

Unfortunately, Long was not given the full measure of credit for his discovery until much later. At the time, he was accused of being a hypnotist, a master of voodoo, and even a charlatan.[1]

GEORGIA'S GREAT COMMONER

After the Civil War, two men were revered by both the North and the South. One was General Robert E. Lee. The other was Alexander Hamilton Stephens. Stephens, who served as vice president of the Confederate States of America and as governor of Georgia, stood as a proponent of peace in a time of terrible upheaval. Stephens was never viewed by the North or South as an aggressive Southern radical or "fire eater." Although Stephens opposed Georgia's secession from the Union, he did believe that Georgia had a constitutional right to secede and join the other Confederate States. When asked to serve the Confederacy, he, like General Lee, consented graciously.

However, as vice president of the Confederacy, Stephens constantly challenged President Jefferson Davis's decisions and argued for peace at several key points during the war.

Despite Stephens's efforts toward a negotiated peace, the Civil War ended in the South's military defeat. Approximately one month after Lee's surrender, Stephens was arrested at his home in Crawfordville (approximately halfway between Atlanta and Augusta) for serving the Confederacy and was imprisoned in Fort Warren in Boston Harbor.

True to his beliefs, Stephens returned to Georgia upon his release and urged reconciliation between the North and South. On November 15, 1882, "Little Aleck" was inaugurated as governor of the state of Georgia. Unfortunately, less than three months later, he became violently ill and died. Upon his death, his friend Robert Toombs said of him, "More brain and soul and the least flesh of any man I ever knew." Stephens is honored as one of Georgia's entrants in Statuary Hall in the United States Capitol Building. (Another Georgia entrant is Stephens's old college roommate, Crawford W. Long.)

LITTLE ALECK

Stevens was called "Little Aleck" because of his slight stature—he was four feet, ten inches tall and weighed less than one hundred pounds.

Shucking the Corn

When Stephens and President Lincoln met to attempt negotiations in 1865, Stephens arrived bundled under many layers of clothing. Lincoln reportedly joked with his diminutive companion, "Mr. Stephens, you are the smallest nubbin I ever saw to have so many shucks."

ATLANTA'S MOST UNWELCOME GUEST

William Tecumseh Sherman seemed to fail at everything he tried except military service. Born in Ohio in 1820, he was one of eleven children. He graduated from West Point along with many of the Southern officers against whom he eventually fought. In 1853, he resigned from military service and became a banker for a time. He failed at that profession. He took up practicing law in Kansas; he was unsuccessful. He became a superintendent at a military school in Louisiana; he failed at that. He then moved on to become president of a St. Louis streetcar company, but with no success. After a string of disappointments, Sherman returned to military life, accepting an appointment as an infantry colonel in 1861. The Civil War became Sherman's route to success.

General W. T. Sherman

Sherman was sent first to Kentucky to hold that state for the Union, and later actively participated in the Battles of Shiloh, Chickasaw Bluff, Vicksburg, and Chattanooga. Eventually his progress came to the attention of General Ulysses S. Grant, supreme commander of the Union Army, who designated him leader of a force that would crush both Atlanta and Georgia.

General Sherman was bound, bent, and determined to break the Southern will, and he knew he had to have Atlanta to defeat the Confederacy. He intended to deprive the entire South of both physical and psychological sustenance. Sherman therefore looked to the railroad system when he planned his strategy; he would surround and isolate the city, then systematically destroy each railroad that supported Atlanta.

The Battle of Atlanta began with heavy shelling on July 22, 1864, and ended forty days later, when Atlantans were forced to evacuate the city. Sherman took the city and stayed for two months. During this time, he completed his plans for his historic March to the Sea. On November 15, 1864, he and 62,000 men set out to cut a forty-mile-wide swath through Georgia. Anything that could fuel the war machine of the South—railroads, public buildings, manufacturing plants, crops, war supplies—was destroyed. The destruction began with the burning of Atlanta itself. (See chapter 2.)

Onlookers described the city as "flame wrapped," and a "hell on earth." The greatest flames came from the Atlanta Gas Light Factory near today's Georgia World Congress Center. (This is the firestorm depicted in *Gone With the Wind* when Scarlett leaves Atlanta en route to Jonesboro.)

Did Sherman · DO IT? ·

There *is* some controversy over whether Sherman ordered the burning of Atlanta. We do not know if Sherman issued the order to torch the city, but we do know that his army was allowed to run wild and that an abundant supply of whiskey fueled the conflagration of Atlanta. Some say his soldiers—who had fought so hard to conquer the city—believed that they had earned the right to destroy it.

SHERMAN'S FIRST LOVE

Sherman was not only a man of war, but also a man of his word. While a student at West Point, he met Cecilia Stovall, a true Georgia belle.

He courted her and by some accounts was quite smitten. Sadly for Sherman, she hardly gave him the time of day, and returned to Georgia to marry a man named Charles Shellman. Years later, on his March to the Sea, Sherman sought out her Georgia home and knocked on her door. The servant who answered her door was upset that "Yankees" were on the veranda. Upon seeing Sherman and his men, she reportedly moaned, "What will Miss Cecilia do if they burn her house!" Certain that it was the Cecilia he had known long ago, Sherman ordered his soldiers to spare the house. Then Sherman scribbled a note to Cecilia:

> *Madame, you once said that you would hate to be my enemy. I replied that I would protect you even if you were. This I have done. Forgive all else. I am but a soldier.* [2]

SOUTHERN HOSPITALITY

If there is one Atlantan responsible for the positive publicity given to the city after the Civil War, it is Henry Woodfin Grady. To date, no one has done more to sing the praises of "The New South," a term he coined, than this man. The editor of the

Atlanta Constitution, Grady attracted national attention and admiration with his postwar newspaper coverage of the South and his city.

Grady is best known for his December 21, 1886, speech in New York. He was invited to address the New England Society at Delmonico's Restaurant, and Grady knew that one of the other attendees would be the South's nemesis, William Tecumseh Sherman. Sherman, too, had become an after-dinner speaker, and he often discussed his role in the Civil War in his speeches.

As part of Grady's address, he spoke directly to Sherman:

> *I want to say to General Sherman, who is considered an able man in our parts, but kind of careless with fire, that from the ashes he left us in 1864, we have built a brave and beautiful city in Atlanta, that we have caught the sunshine in the brick and mortar of our homes, and have built therein not one ignoble prejudice or memory.*

Interrupted thirty times by applause, Grady's proud speech echoed around the world.

Grady tirelessly promoted Atlanta and the New South. After the Civil War, he also became a strong proponent of large exhibitions that allowed cities to show off their wares. He believed it essential that Atlanta stage one or more such exhibitions, and he was such a good salesman for the city that the Federal Government donated $200,000 for staging the first exposition, held in 1881. It was a big affair, attracting more than one million visitors to Atlanta.

The Liberty Bell was brought from Philadelphia; President Grover Cleveland and Booker T. Washington of Tuskegee Institute both gave speeches. Visitors even saw a demonstration of cotton being picked, processed, and made into a suit, right before their eyes.

Just eleven days before Grady died, he lectured in Boston on "Race Problems in the South." When Grady passed away on December 23, 1889, thousands came to his funeral; the *New York Times* reported that no private person was ever so universally mourned.

A statue memorializing Grady was unveiled on October 21, 1891; Grady Hospital, Grady County, Henry Grady High School, and Henry Grady School of Journalism at the University of Georgia are all present-day testimonies to the great respect held for Grady and his memory.

The Henry W. Grady Monument, as pictured on a 1952 postcard.

ATLANTA'S FIRST AFRICAN-AMERICAN MILLIONAIRE

Through his wise investments and generous contributions to charity, Alonzo Herndon established himself as one of the most prominent and best-loved entrepreneurs in the city. Herndon, the son of a white slave owner and a slave, became Atlanta's first black millionaire.

In 1878, when Herndon was almost twenty years old, he decided to seek his fortune. He left his mother, brother, and the life of a sharecropper behind with only eleven dollars in his pocket. He hired himself out to a man in Conyers, and in six months he managed to save fifty of the sixty dollars total pay he had earned.

Herndon then moved to Jonesboro and paid a barber six dollars a month to teach him the trade. (Barbering was one of the few personal services blacks were allowed to perform for whites at that time.) Although Herndon only had twelve months of formal schooling, he was intelligent, hard working, and willing to wait for his hard work to pay off.

Eventually Herndon moved to Atlanta, and by 1902 he had saved enough money to buy a first-class barber shop at 66 Peachtree Street. In 1905, Herndon was able to purchase a small "burial association" for $140. Burial associations, organized by churches or private groups, were early versions of insurance providers. Herndon later bought nine other such associations. This group of associations became the nucleus for Atlanta Mutual Insurance Company, later called the Atlanta Life Insurance Company. Atlanta Life provided insurance to low-income black families, mortgages to those blacks who had been refused financing by banks, and white-collar jobs to members of the black community.

THE HERNDON HOUSE AND THE TRAGIC DEATH OF ADRIENNE HERNDON

Adrienne Herndon, the accomplished Shakespearean actress who became the wife of Alonzo Herndon, was instrumental in creating a monument to black upper-class life at the turn of the century.

As the Herndon's wealth grew, the couple decided to build a grand mansion on a one-acre plot of land on the edge of Atlanta University. (In fact, the university owned the land for several years after the house was built.) Influenced by her world travels and love of the arts, Adrienne Herndon selected a striking Beaux Arts design for her home. The building permit was issued in 1908, and the couple hired black craftsmen to construct the house. The magnificent fifteen-room, 6,000-square-foot mansion contained numerous personal touches, including a mural in the living room depicting Alonzo Herndon's life.

Sadly, just as her dream home was being completed, Adrienne Herndon fell ill with Addison's disease, an adrenal gland disorder marked by weakness, anemia, weight loss, tanning of the skin, and sometimes nervousness and irritability. At that time, there was no cure for the disease, and her condition rapidly declined. She lived in the completed home only a few days before she died on April 6, 1910, leaving behind a grieving husband and a thirteen-year-old son.

Alonzo Herndon remarried two years later, taking Chicago hairdresser and manicurist Jessie Gillespie as his wife. When Herndon died in 1927, Atlanta Life Insurance Company had assets exceeding one million dollars. Today, Atlanta Life Insurance Company is the second largest black-owned insurance company in the United States. Before Norris Herndon died in 1977, he made provisions for the Herndon home to be opened as a memorial to his parents. It stands today, open to the public, near the campus of Morris Brown College.[3]

THE VENABLE BROTHERS AND THEIR DOUBLE-SIDED LEGACY

Stone Mountain, now a state park, is undoubtedly Atlanta's most striking natural landmark. In Atlanta's early days, the mountain was privately owned, and the granite from its quarries supported one of the leading industries of Georgia.

Samuel and William Venable, two Atlanta brothers, purchased the mountain in 1887 for $48,000. According to family members, the Venables were involved with the founding of the "Knights of Mary Phagan," the Klan organization inspired by Mary Phagan's murder. (See chapter 7.) The brothers also led the renewal of Klan activities in 1915. Throughout the 1920s and 30s, the Venables allowed the Klan to burn crosses at the top of the mountain on each Labor Day. The National Knights of the Ku Klux Klan moved their ceremonies to the outskirts of Stone Mountain Village in 1946.

The brothers also donated the steep side of Stone Mountain to be used for a Confederate memorial carving. The Venables feared that one day the Confederacy would be lost, forgotten, and hated, and they hoped the memorial would help future generations remember the men who fought and died for "The Cause."

This 1952 postcard of the design model for the Stone Mountain Memorial Carving hints at the scale of the original plans for the monument.

Start to finish, the carving took fifty-five years and three artists to complete. Naturally, there were conflicts along the way. The Venables were unhappy with some of the features in the emerging monument:

Completed design model — Confederate Memorial — Stone Mountain, Ga.
Memorial will be 138 ft. high and ¼ mi. long

K5533

they were concerned that the noses of the horses were Roman rather than the proper quarter; the bridles looked all wrong; and, worst of all, the men were riding with their hats off, something real soldiers would never do!

The original plan was to feature Confederate officers, the cavalry, artillery, and infantry stretching across, or perhaps even around, the mountain. The finished work features only a portion of the envisioned sculpture: General Robert E. Lee, Confederate President Jefferson Davis, and General Thomas Jonathan "Stonewall" Jackson ride alone across the north face of Stone Mountain. The work is the largest relief sculpture in the world.

MR. IMPERIAL WIZARD

James R. Venable, former Imperial Wizard, was undoubtedly the most visible member of the Invisible Empire, or the National Knights of the Ku Klux Klan. Unlike his more discreet uncles, who had revived the Klan in 1915, James openly displayed his affinity for white robes. A lawyer who defended everyone from two men accused of bombing the Jewish Temple to Black Muslims, Venable claimed that he was for equal— albeit very separate—rights for all races.

Venable spent thousands of dollars of his own money promoting the Klan, yet as an Atlanta lawyer he never billed a single client. He explained, "I tell people when I take their case about how much it's going to be. Then, if they pay me, it's okay, and if they don't, that's okay too."

Venable became a target of the Federal Bureau of Investigation, which tried unsuccessfully for many years to disbar him. Finally, age took care of what the government could not. In 1989, at the age of 87,

Venable agreed to surrender his license just before a hearing to disbar him on the grounds of senility. It was widely reported for years that Venable often fell asleep during trials.

When Venable died in January, 1993, his family scheduled the funeral services on the exact same day and at the same time as Bill Clinton's Presidential Inauguration, yet the efforts to divert media attention away from Venable's funeral only partially worked. A determined news crew showed up on the scene looking for men in white robes, but the only one they found was Venable's nephew, Reverend Jerry Light—he was a minister wearing his liturgical gown.

PROFESSOR BASS'S SWITCHES

The Atlanta public school system, established in 1869, grew by the day. Modern pedagogical methods were employed along with vigorously enforced old-fashioned punishment. Any infraction prompted the use of the switch.

Professor W. A. Bass, a teacher for many years at Boys' High, was quite a believer in this form of punishment and known far and wide for his "switchins." *A Brief History of the Atlanta Public School System* (1922) had this to say about Professor Bass:

> [He] had a farm out in the country, to which he went every Friday afternoon. When he came back Monday morning, he came with a large bundle of switches, good lithe switches. He laid them on a little shelf about his door, in full sight of his class. By the

next Friday afternoon his switches were all used up; and Monday morning he would bring in another supply. Professor Bass was not only efficient with the switch, but the way he would shake a boy was a plenty. He would take the boy by the lapels of his coat and nearly shake him to pieces; at least that's what the boy thought at the time.[4]

One boy who grew up to be a prominent citizen of Atlanta (and whose daughter grew up to write the novel *Gone With the Wind*), got a whipping on his very first day of high school. Eugene Mitchell also grew up to "turn the tables" on Professor Bass. Mitchell became president of the Atlanta Board of Education. In addition to his ensuring that students had the finest education possible, he also saw to it that corporal punishment was abolished from the Atlanta public schools.

LOVE IS IN THE AIR

Probably the best known of all Atlanta pilots was Douglas Henry Davis. He was one of the firsts in the emerging field of aviation; in fact, the Wright Brothers were his flight instructors.

Davis's story is inexorably linked to that of Glenna Mae D'Hollosy. Davis fell in love at first sight with Glenna Mae and married her on December 25, 1925. They stepped out of the church and into Doug Davis's waiting airplane.

Glenna Mae tells the story of a late-afternoon flight to Stone Mountain after their marriage. "He [Doug Davis] insisted that I go with him one day and fly over Stone Mountain. I think he wanted to show me something, but I can't remember what. Anyway, it got late in the day, and dark, too. Planes back then didn't have any lights, and, of course, there were no lighted airports. So, we were flying along, it was twilight, and I noted that all of the cars below seemed to be stopped, lined up with their lights on, all pointing toward the airport. It was a curious show.

"When we got back to the airport," she adds, "someone told us that the people of Atlanta had seen us up late in evening and thought we were a plane in trouble. So they had organized a light brigade to show us the way to the airport. They didn't know Doug Davis knew that runway in the dark! I think maybe the plane could have landed itself!"

PARACHUTING CANDY

World War I was over, but Davis wanted to put his aviation skills to good use. For a while he worked for the makers of a famous candy bar, dropping the treats from his plane to waiting children below. (Concerned about the velocity of the falling candy, Davis also designed small parachutes for the candy bars!)

Around 1926, Doug Davis started Davis Air Service on the Candler Racetrack, and later built the first hangar at the newly formed Atlanta Municipal Airport. "He knew from the start that Atlanta would be a great airport," says Glenna Mae.

Davis established quite a name for himself. As an aviation pioneer, he set speed records and won numerous national competitions. Davis was also the first captain for Eastern Air Transport, originally known as Pitcairn Aviation. According to Miss Glenna Mae, two days after he accepted this position, he was approached by "two of his crop-dusting buddies from Mississippi who wanted him for the same thing. They were starting a new airline." Davis explained that he had taken the position with Eastern Air, but offered his hangar crew. They went off to form Delta Air Lines.

The love story between Doug and Glenna Mae ended suddenly on Labor Day, 1934. Davis was flying that day in the National Air Races in Cleveland, Ohio. The morning flights went well. The afternoon was tragic. "He didn't want to fly the plane they wanted him to fly," says Miss Glenna Mae. "He believed that the engines were too powerful for the wings. But he didn't want to disappoint the crowds, so he flew." Doug Davis perished in a plane crash just a few hours after he had broken the existing speed record (304.98 miles per hour). He left behind a daughter, a son, and a loving wife.[5]

AVIATION IN ATLANTA

William Berry Hartsfield made Atlanta a center of commercial aviation almost single-handedly. A lawyer by trade, Hartsfield was an aviation visionary by vocation, using his influence and intellect to push Atlanta to the forefront of the burgeoning aviation field.

Born in 1890, he dropped out of Boys' High School his senior year. While clerking at a prestigious law firm, he took it upon himself to write the deans of several top law schools. He asked them what books they would recommend for someone like him who had dropped out of high school. He went on to inform them that he would like to go to college and law school, but just could not afford it. The deans responded, and Hartsfield read every book on their list. He passed the Georgia Bar in 1917, and began his practice in 1921.

When Hartsfield won his first election as alderman, he was named chairman of the supposedly do-nothing aviation committee. The enthusiastic new chairman quickly changed the committee's reputation, immediately jumping into the search for the site of a city airport. With Doug Davis's assistance, Hartsfield decided that the Candler Racetrack was the best possible location, and persuaded the Atlanta City Council to lease and then buy the land.

Then Hartsfield had to tackle the problems of limited funds and unsophisticated materials. John Grey, the first official Atlanta airport manager, had at his disposal two mules, two wagons, six men, and $300 in his construction budget. Fifty chain-gang prisoners and a steam shovel were used to grade and extend two landing strips.

Air routes were still being developed. There was no flying by instruments, and landings took place on rough dirt strips. Pilots had to abide by visual flight rules which were being written and revised with each flight. The Air Commerce Act of 1926 established airmail service from New York to Miami and from New York to San Francisco. For navigation and safety, the routes included high-powered beacons every ten miles to mark the route. Pilots kept on track by flying beacon to beacon. Word got out that Birmingham, Alabama, rather than Atlanta would be the beacon stop on the north-south line below the Appalachian Mountains. Given Hartsfield's ultimate plan, this possibility could not become reality. He set out to change the government's mind.

Hartsfield arranged for the governor of Georgia,

the mayor of Atlanta, and other Atlanta businessmen to issue an invitation to the assistant secretary of commerce for aeronautics. Upon his arrival, the visiting official was given VIP treatment, a motorcycle escort throughout Atlanta, a banquet, and a full compliment of high-level meetings. Anyone who was worth meeting met with the assistant secretary. One week later Atlanta was chosen over Birmingham for the route.

In 1930 Atlanta Municipal Airport handled sixteen passenger and airmail flights a day. A new terminal was built in 1931; proceeds raised by selling $2.50 plane rides over Stone Mountain paid for the terminal's furniture. Under Hartsfield's tutelage, lighted runways, the nation's first air passenger terminal, an air control tower, and an instrument landing system eventually were added to the growing airport.

Hartsfield, the father of Atlanta aviation, was rewarded for his prowess and elected mayor of Atlanta. Atlanta's international airport is named in honor William B. Hartsfield.

A NEW KING

Dr. Martin Luther King, Jr.'s lifework for civil rights reached far beyond the borders of Atlanta, but his death brought him back to his hometown. Dr. King was assassinated on April 4, 1968. After news of the assassination broke on television, riots erupted in cities across the country. Fortunately a heavy rain fell in Atlanta, keeping people off the streets.

Hoping the peace would hold, Mayor Ivan Allen, Jr., and Police Chief Herbert Jenkins spent four hours that day visiting every black neighborhood in Atlanta to express sorrow and concern. That night, all was quiet. There was no violence in King's hometown.

Although things were calm, there was still the fear that racist whites would stir up trouble. The mayor had received several telegrams from such people suggesting the city ignore the funeral. Governor Lester Maddox scoffed at

Little
· MIKE ·

Today, Martin Luther King, Jr., is a household name. In 1929, that famous name existed only in the mind of his dying grandfather. The owner of the most famous name in the history of American civil rights was born January 15, 1929, and named "Michael Luther King, Jr.," after his father. But as he was dying, Michael Junior's grandfather, James Albert King, asked his son Michael to change his first name to Martin. Then he said, "Change Little Mike's, too." When his grandson was five years old, his name was legally changed to Martin Luther King, Jr., just as his grandfather had wished.

the plans to lower flags in Atlanta to half-mast. He would spend the funeral in his office with the blinds drawn and surrounded by about one hundred members of the Georgia State Patrol. They were ready to protect Governor Maddox should racial tensions erupt into violence. In contrast, hundreds of white churches announced they would open their doors to black visitors, offering comfort to grief-stricken followers of Dr. King.

The memorial services attracted politicians and celebrities from across the country. Jacqueline Kennedy, Bobby Kennedy, Richard Nixon, Nelson Rockefeller, Harry Belafonte, Wilt Chamberlain, James Brown, and many, many more attended. Although only 800 people could fit inside Ebenezer Baptist Church for the actual funeral service, some 200,000 mourners marched along with the funeral procession from the church to Morehouse College. Following the mule-drawn wagon bearing the casket, the grieving crowd sang choruses of "We Shall Overcome."

> Following Martin Luther King's death, forty-six people were killed in rioting in 126 cities across the United States. Atlanta was untouched by violence.

HAMMERIN' HANK

One would think that 1973 and 1974 were the greatest years in Henry Aaron's life, because during that time the Atlanta Braves slugger Hank Aaron was closing in on the home run record set by Babe Ruth. Instead, those years were filled with terror. Death threats came practically every day. (Aaron recalled many of them in his autobiography, *I Had A Hammer*.)

At a news conference honoring the twentieth anniversary of his home run record, Aaron said, "God

gave me the talent to play the game. I was not going to let people take that away from me by writing letters. I was not going to stand by and let people threaten me."[6]

Aaron saved every single one of the "hate" letters. When one contained a specific threat, Braves management placed the note in a plastic bag and turned it over to the FBI. After the threats became public knowledge, a torrent of positive, supportive mail flooded in from well-wishers.

April 8, 1974, was the day Aaron broke Babe Ruth's home run record, hitting magic number 715. The Braves were at home playing the Dodgers, with Al Downing as the opposing pitcher. Aaron came up to bat in the fourth inning, and on the second pitch he hit the ball over the left-field fence into the bullpen. As Aaron rounded the bases, two University of Georgia students vaulted over the railing and ran along side him. The duo were criticized for ruining Aaron's moment of glory, but Aaron did not seem to mind. Braves pitcher Tom House found the ball and ran over to present it to the jubilant Aaron. Aaron writes that he keeps the ball in a bank vault.

The Atlanta Braves won the 1995 World Series in the same stadium that witnessed Hank Aaron's amazing feats. Unfortunately, this stadium will soon be history itself. It is scheduled to be torn down and replaced with a new stadium.

Hank's · SPOT ·

Today, a sign at Atlanta-Fulton County Stadium marks the historic spot where number 715 was hit out of the park.

4

LAW

» »AND «‹ «‹

DISORDER

·4·

Law and Disorder

BOVINE LAWS

Post-Civil War Atlanta was not a one-horse town, but it still had pastures. Police officers not only had to contend with criminals, but they also had to deal with a growing population of stray animals. The animal problem became so big that the Atlanta City Council passed the "1875 Cow Ordinance." The law

Why So Many · COWS? ·

Atlanta did not have commercial dairies in 1875, and locals had to keep their own cows if they wanted milk.

required that farm animals be kept in a pen at night. (What happened to them by day is uncertain.) A fine of two dollars was levied for each captured cow. The law also beseeched anyone who saw a stray heifer to participate in the roundup. Most locals, however, merely watched while the police chased the delinquent cows.

Judge Hopkins repeatedly violated this ordinance; his cow was regularly found loitering on the sidewalk. One evening Officer Monaghan found the beast lounging in the right of way. The good officer began to shoo Judge Hopkins's cow out of the way when suddenly the tables were turned. Instead of the policeman herding the cow, the cow sent the officer running for the nearest tree. After several rounds of advance and retreat, the officer finally succeeded in penning up the cow. From that point on, Officer Monaghan was known throughout Atlanta for his prowess with "dumb" animals.

CHAIN GANGS

After the Civil War, a reconstruction government, composed mainly of Yankees trying to take advantage of the vanquished city (carpetbaggers) and Southerners who allied themselves with the Yankees (scalawags), controlled Georgia and Atlanta. Nevertheless, the city grew and prospered. Unfortunately, the growth in size was accompanied by an increase in crime. The reconstruction government faced a serious problem: what to do with convicted criminals.

Sherman had destroyed the state's penitentiary. There was no funding for the housing or care of criminals. To many people, feeding criminals seemed a waste of good—and scarce—money. Confronted with these obstacles, the reconstruction government

opposite:
The car shed of
the Western and
Atlantic Depot.

came up with a creative solution to the prisoner predicament: they could hire out the prisoners to the highest bidder for constructive work in the community.

The convicts were placed in lumber mills, in fields, on railroad repairs or general construction crews—any place where a strong back and a broken spirit could be used. (Even Scarlett O'Hara, *Gone With the Wind*'s heroine, hired them to work in her lumber mills.)

Setting up a convict lease program was the "perfect" solution to the problem. The responsibility and expense of taking care of prisoners now shifted to the privateers who enrolled in the program. The supply of manpower was endless. Any person—male, female, black, white, adult or child—convicted of a felony was up for lease. Even the insane could serve as lessees in this program. The lease program soon became a big business, and big abuses followed. By 1876, three companies held twenty-year leases on almost every state prisoner. When the lease program started, approximately 1,000 prisoners were turned over for use in private business. By 1899 when the lease expired, the number had doubled.

The convicts, ninety percent of whom were African-American, had no advocates and worked fifteen hours a day, seven days a week. They were governed in the field by bosses who frequently whipped and beat them. Food was not plentiful, and many died of starvation and neglect.

Finally, in 1897, former Confederate General John B. Gordon (part owner of one of the companies who leased convicts) spoke out against the program. Governor William Atkinson and the Georgia General Assembly took the first steps toward prison reform. The convict lease camps were abolished in 1908. But the "chain gang," a close cousin of the convict lease program, still exists in some parts of the United States.

JIM CROW

Before the turn of the turn of the century, the Georgia Assembly passed laws that segregated blacks and whites. These laws earned the nickname "Jim Crow laws" after an old minstrel song titled, "Jump, Jim Crow." The term "Jim Crow" can apply to any written or customary rule that keeps the races separate. One law passed in 1891 required railroads to provide separate passenger cars for each race; streetcar regulations soon followed. Separate theaters, water fountains, beaches, neighborhoods, jobs, elevators, park benches, and military units soon became standard. In both the North and the South, attitudes of white supremacy took hold. While blacks protested strongly, little change occurred. Racial hatred became socially acceptable in some circles.

The magnitude of the racial tensions became obvious on May 16, 1902, when the "Pittsburg Riot" (named after an area in Atlanta) broke out. When the riot was over, three police officers and three black citizens were dead and a city block was reduced to ashes.

THE 1906 RACE RIOTS

The one-night Pittsburgh Riot paled in comparison to the four-day, full-fledged riot that hit Atlanta four years later. The 1906 Race Riots were triggered by a heated gubernatorial battle between Hoke Smith, former president and owner of the *Journal,* and Clark Howell, former editor of the *Constitution.* Smith's platform promised a constitutional amendment which would take the vote away from African-

Americans. Tom Watson, as caustic and vitriolic as ever, supported Smith. (See chapters 3 and 7.) Smith won. The heated campaign left tempers running high.

On September 22, 1906, sensationalized stories of four alleged attempted assaults by black men on white women appeared in the press. That evening, an enraged crowd gathered at the intersection of Pryor and Decatur Streets. For no apparent reason, drunken white youths attacked a black bicycle messenger. He was rescued by the police, but it was too late to stop the riot that was to occur. The mob grew to include over 2,000 people. Before the fire department hoses could cool off hotheads, African-American citizens were chased and pulled off trolleys. Even the chief-of-police himself engaged in hand-to-hand combat.

After four days of bedlam, ten African-Americans and two whites were dead, sixty African-Americans and ten whites were wounded, and damage to property throughout the city was substantial.

"MAKE GEORGIA A SECOND RENO?"

So read the headline of a 1937 St. Valentine's Day article in the *Atlanta Journal Magazine*. A bill was pending in the state legislature which would give Georgia the most lax divorce laws in the country, requiring only a thirty-day waiting period for a couple to dissolve their marriage. Reno, the reigning divorce capital, had a forty-two-day residency requirement.

State Representative Billy Barrett of Augusta proposed the measure as a way to attract unhappy spouses who might otherwise head to Florida to take advantage of that state's ninety-day waiting period. South Carolina had no divorce laws at all, so Augusta, which sat on the Georgia–South Carolina border, stood to profit substantially from those South Carolinians seeking divorce. The bill never became law, however.

UNTYING THE KNOT

In 1938, Atlantans were shocked to learn that the number of divorces in Fulton County had exceeded the number of weddings. That year, 2,167 marriage certificates were issued in the county, while 2,210 divorce decrees were granted. That left Atlanta's marriage rate in the hole by forty-three.[1]

GEORGIA'S THREE GOVERNORS

Georgia became the laughingstock of the nation in 1947 when two—and then three—governors held office simultaneously. It took court intervention to straighten out the biggest mess that Georgia politics has seen to this day.

Usually, when the November elections came to the state, there was little suspense about the outcome. Whoever won the Democratic primary always won the general election, and in this case, Eugene Talmadge was the only name on the November ballot.

But as election day approached, it became clear to Talmadge's inner circle that the aging and ailing politician might not live through the election. Talmadge's supporters interpreted the new state constitution as allowing the legislature to choose from the next two highest candidates in the general election, should the governor-elect die before taking office. To hedge against this possibility, word went out for Talmadge supporters to write in the name of Talmadge's son, Herman, on the ballot.

Eugene Talmadge won the general election in November. But at 7:00 A.M., Saturday, December 21, 1947, he died without being inaugurated or taking office. The political jockeying started before the body could grow cold.

Outgoing governor Ellis Arnall decided he should stay in office until Melvin Thompson, Georgia's first lieutenant governor, who had also been elected in November, was sworn in and could assume the duties as acting governor. State Attorney General Eugene Cook agreed with Arnall.

The Talmadge cronies in the legislature had other ideas. On January 15, the lawmakers convened and immediately began to examine the votes from the general election, refusing to admit they might not have the authority to elect a governor. Talmadge supporters were in for a shock when they discovered that Eugene's son Herman Talmadge had come in *third* in spite of the vigorous write-in campaign. Then seventy-seven votes mysteriously arrived from Telfair County, moving Talmadge into second place. (These votes supposedly were found misfiled in the lieutenant governor's office.) That was all the legislature needed. Herman Talmadge was elected on the spot and inaugurated immediately.

After giving a very brief inaugural address, Talmadge marched downstairs to move into his new office. The door was locked, so Talmadge and his staff battered it down. Governor Arnall and one of his staff members were inside and refused to budge. Talmadge backed off, but it turned out to be only a temporary retreat. Arnall finally felt it was safe to leave at 3:30 A.M., but when he returned later that morning, he found all the locks changed and Talmadge in charge. Arnall had been kicked out of the governor's office, but he refused to leave the building, setting up shop instead in the capitol rotunda. Arnall was later evicted from the governor's mansion when Talmadge, his twenty-three-year-old wife Betty and their two boys moved in.

Sitting on
· THE SEAL ·

During these months of confusion, little state business had been accomplished. This was not entirely due to the general inability to discern who was in charge, but in part because "The Great Seal of Georgia" was missing from the safe. Secretary of State Ben Fortson had doubts about Talmadge's legal right to the governor's office and wanted to insure that the courts, rather than the politicians, had the last say in the matter. Afraid someone might break into the safe at night to steal the symbol of state power, Fortson took the seal himself and hid it in his wheelchair. Fortson said, "I sat on the seal by day and slept on it by night. If you don't believe it leaves a lasting impression, try that for sixty-three days."[2] When the governor crisis ended, the seal reappeared.

On January 18th, the third governor entered the fray. Melvin Thompson was sworn in as lieutenant governor and thus as the state's acting governor. At this point, Arnall, the outgoing governor, stepped aside to let Thompson take charge. But Talmadge still refused to give up possession of the office or his position in the governor's mansion. Thompson then decided to turn to the courts to settle the dispute.

The first ruling on the matter came from Judge Walter Hendrix of Fulton Superior Court. He dismissed a suit filed by Thompson and ruled that Talmadge was the legal governor. A three-judge panel in McDonough concurred: Talmadge was governor. Attorney General Cook appealed to the Georgia Supreme Court. It took over two months for a ruling.

Sixty-three days after the whole thing started, the court ruled that M. E. Thompson was the rightful and legal governor of Georgia. Talmadge chose not to fight the decision, and within forty-five minutes he had cleared out his desk and left the capitol.

Georgia voters had not heard the last of Herman Talmadge, however. Two years later, he ran against Thompson and won.

BLACK, WHITE, AND ASSORTED COLORS

"We are a city too busy to hate. It's the pattern of modern Atlanta. Our aim in life is to make no business, no industry, no educational or social organization ashamed of…'Atlanta.'" That's how Mayor William B. Hartsfield summed up his philosophy in an interview in *Newsweek* magazine.

Nevertheless, in 1961, as Hartsfield planned his retirement from politics, one more major hurdle remained: the peaceful, though symbolic, desegregation of Atlanta public schools. The world watched

mobs protest integration in Little Rock and New Orleans. Atlanta citizens understood their choice: either obey the Supreme Court order to integrate the schools or shut the schools down entirely.

After rigorous examinations, a small group of black students was selected to attend four formerly all-white Atlanta schools. These students were Madeyln Nix and Thomas Welch, chosen to attend Henry Grady High; Donita Gaines, Arthur Simmons, and Willie Jean Black, who were assigned to Northside High; and Martha Ann Holmes, who was picked to attend Murphy High.

School Superintendent Dr. John Letson urged parents and all Atlantans to accept the inevitable. Police Chief Herbert Jenkins assured parents that their children would be safe. Police were dispatched, ready to handle any problem that came up.

Surprisingly, there were no problems at all. The opening day of school began as any other—except for the fact that history was made. That day, August 30, 1961, President John F. Kennedy praised the quiet integration of the Atlanta schools:

> I want to take this opportunity to congratulate Governor Vandiver, Mayor Hartsfield of Atlanta, Chief of Police Jenkins, Superintendent of Schools Letson, and all of the parents, students and citizens of Atlanta, Georgia, for the responsible law-abiding manner in which four high schools were desegregated today.
>
> This was the result of vigorous efforts for months by the officials of Atlanta and by groups of citizens through the community. Their efforts have borne fruit in the

orderly manner in which the desegregation was carried out with dignity
and without violence and disrespect
for the law.

I strongly urge the officials and
citizens of all communities which face
this difficult transition in the coming
weeks and months to look closely at
what Atlanta has done to meet their
responsibility, as the officials of Atlanta
and Georgia have done, with courage,
tolerance, and above all, with respect
for the law.[3]

5

LOCOMOBILES, BEELER BLEVINS'S FLYING MACHINE, AND OTHER MAD MODES OF TRANSPORT

Locomobiles, Beeler Blevins's Flying Machine, and Other Mad Modes of Transport

SCORCHERS

The bicycling craze hit Atlanta in 1894. The sport became so popular that it seemed everyone wanted to ride. Although many people questioned the propriety of la-dies riding bi-cycles, by 1895 women were al-lowed to cycle. This was the subject of much debate, and some preachers declared that

Satan was behind every woman on a two-wheeler.

Soon bicycle riders took over Peachtree Street. Bike speeders, or "scorchers," made it nearly impossible for the pedestrians of Atlanta to cross safely to the other side of the street. As a result, in 1896, biking rules were adopted for the wheelmen (and women) of Atlanta.

(1) Keep to the right of the road. Never neglect this.

(2) Request permission of pedestrians for the right-of-way.

(3) Turn to one side for heavy load, even if you are on the right side.

(4) Be ever ready to assist a female rider in distress on the road, even without the formality of an introduction.

(5) Don't scorch, and this means you!

(6) Ride no faster than an eight-mile-an-hour gait in passing through villages where you are unfamiliar with the ordinances. It will save you money.

(7) Lastly, don't say, "Get out of my way" to any chance pedestrian who may appear in your path.[1]

LOCOMOBILES

Every fad has its day, and the cycling craze of the late nineteenth century soon gave right-of-way to the "locomobile." In 1897 (although some sources say as late as 1901), bicycle-dealer J. W. Alexander became the first Atlantan to own a "horseless carriage." Actually, what he bought was a set of three, 650-pound, steam-driven "locomobiles." The contraptions had no lamps and no tops; they were merely buggies with a boiler under the seat and the engine on the axle.

To show off his new toy, Alexander set out on a spectacular round-trip to East Point. Three miles outside of Atlanta, however, the trip came to an unexpected end. A mule that decided it did not like sharing the road with the locomobile simply kicked the car out of its way, sending machine and driver into a nearby ditch. This gives J. W. Alexander the dubious honor of becoming the first Atlanta motorist involved in an auto accident.

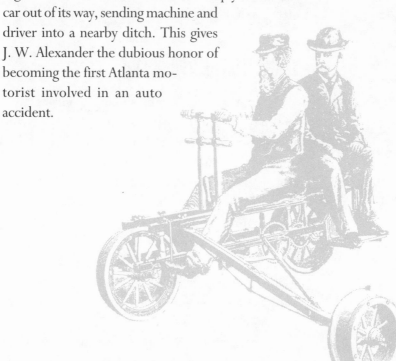

HUSTLING, BUSTLING ATLANTA

By 1900, Atlanta had managed to become the third largest business railhead in the United States. The Atlanta police force included 150 law enforcement officers. The Candler Building was a showplace with its amazing seventeen stories. The expression, "as tall as the Candler Building" became part of the slang of the times, and children from rural areas came to Atlanta just to ride the building's elevators. The Atlanta and Edgewood Street Railway Company transported commuters in from the suburbs. The "Electric Street Dummies," as the streetcars were called, were yellow with gold trim and sported oaken interiors and cane bottom chairs. It only took fifteen minutes to make the trip from downtown to the eastern suburbs. (But the suburbs were much closer to the metro area then!)

TO GET TO THE OTHER SIDE

From the city's very beginning, Atlanta has been known for its traffic jams. In the mid-1850s, as many as a dozen train tracks straddled the streets, and trains—sometimes several at a time—blocked grade crossings at Whitehall and Pryor Streets almost continuously. Since the trains were laid out east and west, travel from north to south often came to a standstill. As a result, horses pulling every imaginable conveyance, their drivers, and pedestrians clogged the streets waiting for the trains to pass. It was not unusual to sit and wait a half hour for the engines, boxcars, and passenger cars to chug by.

There were other problems with the trains, as well. First, the "sewer of cinder smoke" from the trains kept people who lived or worked near the tracks

constantly struggling to clean away the dull residue left by the smoke. Moreover, cinders in the eyes were painful and could cause serious damage to residents' eyesight. The loud noise from the trains was a nuisance; constant train rumblings were a source of irritation among locals.

There had to be a way to bypass the crossings of the Southern Railway, the Seaboard Coast Line Railroad, the Central of Georgia Railroad, the Georgia Railroad, and the Western and Atlantic Railroad. At first, Joel Hurt proposed building a bridge over the tracks in 1875, but the city fathers voted his proposal down as too costly.

On December 31, 1899, Mayor James G. Woodward acknowledged that the time had come to address the traffic problem immediately, and Hurt's proposal was reintroduced and plans for a bridge were approved. At 1:08 P.M., October 9, 1901, Street Car No. 106 with Jerome Simmons, motorman, and H. M. Atkinson, Jr., conductor, reached the middle of Atlanta's first viaduct. Other viaducts were soon built.

Horsecars, dummy lines, trolley cars, jitneys, and later motor buses, taxis, and personal vehicles benefited from the bridges that stretched over the train tracks of Atlanta. Two other benefits occurred as well, but by accident. As new traffic patterns developed, neglected areas of town became

A Free RIDE

•

Mr. James Key, the first man to cross the first viaduct, got the ride for free; the conductor was so excited, he forgot to collect the three-cent fare!

•

prosperous and beneath the viaducts a subterranean city slowly developed.

By 1929, the number of bridges effectively sealed off the railroad crossings, creating a tunnel-like area around Old Alabama Street that was left untouched for decades. Today, reopened as the shopping complex Underground Atlanta, this "subterranean" site is a bustling, energetic part of the city. But remember—Underground is not really *under* ground. Atlanta is just above it!

DIXIE'S CAR

George Washington Hanson was the tinkering type. He dabbled in farming, built bicycles, and even sold insurance. But his first love was the automobile. He was perfect for the newly emerging car sales industry; he spent over ten years selling the E-M-F, the Studebaker, and the Franklin. Eventually, he decided to build a car of his own—the "Southern Car for the South," with "Made in Dixie" emblazoned on the grill, and the Cotton Boll insignia on the radiator. He constructed "Hanson's Six" entirely from aluminum except for the "Continental" engine and the linoleum fenders. All leather upholstery guaranteed a luxurious feel, and spiffy side curtains maintained privacy.

The Hanson Six made its debut at the Southeastern Auto Show in February, 1917, sold for $1685 and weighed 2,700 pounds. Nine hundred Hanson Six cars were made. There was just one problem; a Ford sold for much less than a Hanson. Henry Ford's 1919 prices were $525 for a touring car, $500 for a runabout; $775 for a sedan, and $650 for a coupelet.

A build-your-own Ford was much less, at $475. The cost difference between the two companies' cars caused the Hanson Six's demise in 1924.

THE BALLOON "CONSPIRACY"

Atlantans learned early to look to the skies for excitement. On December 10, 1889, five thousand Atlantans crowded onto Marietta Street to catch a glimpse of the new air age. At about 2:30 in the afternoon, Dr. Albert Hape and Professor Samuel A. King floated over the area in their new toy, a hot-air balloon.

As if a "flying contraption" over Atlanta wouldn't attract enough attention, Professor King played religious hymns on his bugle as the balloon passed over a revival meeting. (It scared many of the parishioners—they thought the angel Gabriel was playing their song.)

Other balloon watchers had different explanations. The more paranoid of them thought the balloon might be a new way for revenue agents to discover illegal moonshine stills. Another speculated that the balloon was just another way for the notorious governor Rufus Bullock to escape with government funds.

A DAY AT THE RACES

Soon balloons gave way to a more sophisticated form of air travel: the airplane. In the early 1900s, people came to Atlanta from miles around to see the newfangled flying machines gracefully go through their paces. And the best place to see the airplanes in action was the racetrack.

In 1909, the parcel of land on which Hartsfield International Airport is now located was known as Candler Racetrack or Candler Field. It was a popular spot, and Sunday afternoons found the bleachers full of people watching automobile and motorcycle races. Race car drivers thrilled grandstand patrons and inevitably kept them on the edge of their seats.

In between the races, the "new" airplanes used the middle of the speedway as a landing strip. Those up for a bit of adventure could hop in pilot Beeler Blevins's biplane for an exhilarating ride over Atlanta. This ride of a lifetime only cost five dollars.

LONE EAGLE

On October 11, 1927, Charles A. Lindbergh flew into town, symbolizing Atlanta's emerging reputation as a major aviation center. Glenna Mae Davis recounted the Lone Eagle's visit almost seven decades later as if it had happened the day before. (For more on Glenna Mae Davis, see chapter 3.)

"It was an overcast day," Miss Glenna Mae began. "It had been raining. We could hear Lindbergh's plane a long time before he arrived. Visibility was low, and Atlanta was cloudy, with thick gray clouds. He was above the clouds; we kept hearing his engines, wondering when he would break through. You know, there wasn't any radar back then, he was flying by the seat of his pants. He only had a compass. Then all of a sudden, Lindbergh broke through the clouds, right where he was supposed to be. He broke through the clouds right above the airport." It was a perfect landing, except for one little problem, Miss Glenna Mae explained. "It had been raining, and the field was muddy. When 'Lindy' got to the end of the end of the runway, he got stuck in the mud. Immediately all of the mechanics rushed out to get him unstuck and pull him in. But that wasn't Lindbergh's way. He jumped right out of the plane, and put his shoulder right up there with all the greasy mechanics. He was just that way. "[2]

After Lindbergh cleaned off the mud, he was taken into the city by motorcade. People lined the streets just to catch a glimpse of the Lone Eagle. "Lindbergh Day" was marked with VIP visits, a banquet, and a speech by "Lucky Lindy" attended by over 20,000 people. Atlanta was so positively taken with Lindbergh that Mayson Avenue, which ran from Peachtree Street to Piedmont, was renamed "Lindbergh Drive."

Prior to Lindbergh's visit, many Atlantans had been against spending money for a new airport. Most thought it just a "newfangled idea," and couldn't see into aviation's future. After "Lucky Lindy's" visit, however, Atlanta changed its mind. (See chapter 3.)

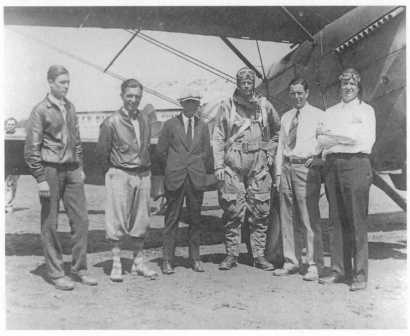

Davis Air Service pilots with
Charles Lindbergh in October 1927,
six months after his record-setting
flight across the Atlantic.
(Lindbergh is third from the right;
Doug Davis is second from the right.)

6

FRANKLY

>> >> M Y << <<

DEAR

·6·

Frankly, My Dear...

STEEPED IN HISTORY

Margaret Mitchell, author of *Gone With the Wind,* was born and raised in Atlanta, and was steeped in the stories of the Confederate past told by her extended family. So steeped, in fact, that Mitchell (known as "Peggy" by her friends) did not know the South had lost the Civil War until she was ten years old, when her mother finally confessed the truth.

Mitchell briefly left the South to go "up north" to attend Smith College, but she returned to Atlanta with all haste when her mother became gravely ill. She did not arrive until the day after her mother's death. (Any fan of *Gone With the Wind* will recognize a parallel in Mitchell's novel; Scarlett O'Hara also arrives at Tara one day too late to tell her mother good-bye.)

Mitchell remained in Atlanta after her mother's death, taking a job with the *Atlanta Journal Sunday*

Magazine, then marrying briefly and unhappily in 1922. Her husband, Berrien K. "Red" Upshaw, disappeared before the first year of marriage ended, and Mitchell won an uncontested divorce in 1924. In 1925, she married the love of her life, John Marsh. One year later, she experienced a lucky break, or rather a lucky sprain, that would change the course of her life.

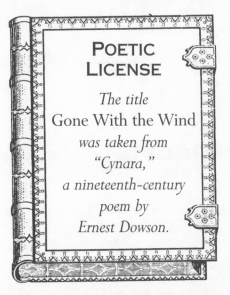

POETIC LICENSE

The title
Gone With the Wind
*was taken from
"Cynara,"
a nineteenth-century
poem by
Ernest Dowson.*

TOMORROW IS ANOTHER DAY

Mitchell sprained an ankle which had been injured twice before, and her convalescence was not an easy one; it took weeks of healing with a cast, traction treatment, and finally crutches. Her husband suggested she stop reading and start writing to help combat her growing restlessness. Mitchell took his advice and started pulling together scattered Civil War stories, connecting them with characters reminiscent of her past.

The manuscript went through a multitude of changes. Scarlett O'Hara began her literary life with the name "Pansy O'Hara"; in fact, "Pansy" was changed to "Scarlett" only six months before publication. "Tara" began as "Fortenoy Hall," while "Melanie Hamilton" narrowly missed being a "Permelia." And somewhere between manuscript and publication, the working title of Mitchell's massive work changed from "Tomorrow Is Another Day" to *Gone With the Wind.*

OUT OF THE CLOSET

In 1935, Macmillan editor Harold Latham came to town on a manuscript-searching tour. He heard about her work, and asked to see it. She demurred, insisting it was not finished. Mitchell wrote years later, "He'd asked for it, and I'd felt very flattered that he even considered me; but I'd refused knowing in what poor shape the thing was."[1]

Even though she had been working on the book for nine years, only a few friends knew about it, and not one had read it or seemed to know what it was about. The manuscript might have remained stuffed in envelopes in her closet if not for the words of a friend who heard she was working on a book.

"Why, are you writing a book, Peggy? How strange you've never said anything about it," said the young woman. She continued, "Well, I daresay. Really, I wouldn't take you for the type who would write a successful book. You know you don't take life seriously enough to be a novelist....But, Peggy, I think you are wasting your time trying. You really aren't the type."[2]

According to Mitchell, these words made her so mad that she grabbed up the pieces of her manuscript and went to see Latham, who was staying at the Georgian Terrace Hotel.

Latham recounted his meeting with Atlanta's Peggy. A few hours before he left Atlanta, the telephone in his hotel room rang and Miss Mitchell's voice came over it informing him that she was downstairs in the lobby and would like to see him. As Latham tells it, "I went down, and I shall never forget the

mental picture that I have of her at that time—a tiny woman sitting on a divan, with the biggest manuscript I have ever seen, towering in two stacks almost to her shoulders."[3]

"Take the *damn* thing before I change my mind," Mitchell said, then quickly departed. When she cooled down the next day, she sent Latham a telegram, "Send it back; I've changed my mind." But it was too late. Latham had read portions of the story and knew it had great potential.

The story went through many changes and revisions before it was published. Her husband John Marsh served as an informal chief editor. At Margaret Mitchell's request, the original manuscript was burned upon her death.

GONE WITH THE WIND, LITERALLY

The Mitchells' last home, the Della Manta Apartments (now known as One South Prado) has the dubious distinction of being the site of the burning of the original *GWTW* manuscript.

WINDFALL

Originally Macmillan planned to publish 10,000 copies. However, when word got out about the subject matter and scope of the book, public demand increased and the book run increased to 50,000 copies. Originally, the highbrow critics panned it, but in one year over one million copies were in print.

In 1937, Margaret Mitchell won the Pulitzer Prize for literature. David O. Selznick paid $50,000, a record amount, for the movie rights. And perhaps most important for Mitchell, Atlantans (and Southerners) in great numbers showed a proprietary kinship and interest in the book.

While she was pleased with the novel's success, Mitchell expressed equal resentment for its intrusion in her home life. There were interests to protect,

Was Scarlett an
· ARIES? ·

Some *Gone With the Wind* buffs (both the novel and film) claim that the characters represent astrological archetypes. One fan claims to have seen Margaret Mitchell's hand-written notes about the creation of her characters with the zodiac in mind. (This same source claims that Mitchell was known as an astrologer in Atlanta during her day.)

Here's how the characters and their signs break down:

Aries: Scarlett O'Hara

Taurus: Scarlett's father, Gerald O'Hara

Gemini: Prissy and Aunt Pitty

Cancer: Melanie Hamilton

Leo: Rhett Butler

Virgo: Scarlett's mother, Miss Ellen

Libra: Belle Watling

Scorpio: Mammy

Sagittarius: Rhett and Scarlett's daughter, Bonnie Butler (This sign is represented by a centaur, and Bonnie is killed riding a horse.)

Capricorn: Ashley Wilkes

Aquarius: Scarlett's second husband, Frank Kennedy

Pisces: Dr. Meade, Careen and Suellen (Scarlett's sisters), and Charles Hamilton, Scarlett's first husband

This same source claims that the Wilkes plantation Twelve Oaks is named for the twelve zodiacal signs.[4]

charlatans to fend off, publication rights to grant, and new rights to negotiate. Then a new tangle of complications resulted during the development of the movie.

FRANKLY, MY DEAR, I *DO* GIVE A DAMN!

Controversy hounded the filming of *GWTW*. One major battle was fought over the most famous line in the film, Rhett's parting line to Scarlett: "Frankly, my dear, I don't give a damn." Many movie fans are surprised to learn that this line is not exactly true to the book. Mitchell's line reads, "My dear, I don't give a damn."

The controversy surrounding this phrase in the movie did not focus on the added word, "frankly," but on the word producer David O. Selznick decided to leave in: "damn." A mild expletive today, at that time the word was considered offensive and shocking, and was strictly prohibited in the movies. Selznick considered the line essential to the film and insisted no substitute would work. (Imagine the line: "Sorry, dear, I just don't care."!) If necessary, Selznick was ready to enlist the help of Georgia's governor and the entire legislature to convince the censors to permit the line. Selznick argued that the word, as used by Rhett Butler, was "not an oath or a vulgarism." Finally, with the help of other industry leaders, a compromise was reached that allowed both sides to save face; Selznick could keep the word in, but he had to pay a $5,000 fine, a word tax.

The movie encountered other problems because of the censor's Production Code of 1933. Selznick was strongly urged to tone down scenes involving marital rape. (Today many people mistake this scene for passion.) He was also required to minimize Belle

Watling's prostitution and Melanie's childbirth scene. Censors would not allow Scarlett to blatantly offer her body to Rhett to raise the money to save Tara. Rhett, Ashley, and the other male characters could not be portrayed as being drunk, and Scarlett could not display too much cleavage or "skin" when she undressed.

Fortunately, Selznick was able to avoid changes that would suck the life out of the film. He did, however, deliberately make one other alteration designed to diffuse racial tension. He excluded mention of the Ku Klux Klan and eliminated the word "nigger" in the movie.

THE HORSE THAT WORE MAKEUP

This is not the actual advertisement, but those *were* the requirements for an animal actor needed for a pivotal scene in *Gone With the Wind.*

> · **CASTING CALL** ·
>
> Horse needed, mare or stallion okay. Must appear to be on the verge of collapse. Has great death scene in new motion picture about the Old South.

Director Victor Fleming needed to cast "Woebegone," the horse Scarlett uses to escape the fires of Atlanta. Five animals of the type once known as "crowbait" were given free trips to the studio in horse trucks. The director discarded each of them as being too prosperous-looking for the part.

Finally, a suitable "Woebegone" was found and cast. Weeks later, on the day the mare was called for her scene, she had gained weight. (Now that she was in the movies, her owners thought the mare could afford to eat.) In fact, she had gained so much weight

that her ribs had disappeared. It was too late to find another horse, so "Woebegone" was quickly ushered into the makeup department.

When she returned to the set, she looked like her movie name. Dark hollows had been painted in her cheeks, while her sides appeared to be deeply furrowed by protruding ribs. Another Hollywood success story!

THE GRAND OLD LADY ON PEACHTREE

Atlanta's movie made its world premiere, fittingly, in Atlanta. Most of the principal film participants started arriving on December 13, 1939. The Georgian Terrace, also known as "The Grand Old Lady on Peachtree," was the only place "fittin' enough" for the *Gone With the Wind* celebrities. Vivien Leigh and her beau Laurence Olivier, Olivia de Havilland, Clark Gable, his wife Carole Lombard, and David O. Selznick all stayed on the ninth floor. Regrettably, during the 1930s there were no integrated hotels in Atlanta. Therefore, Hattie McDaniel, Butterfly McQueen, and other African-American actors were not allowed to attend any of the gala functions nor the premiere. (Ironically, Hattie McDaniel, who played Mammy, won the Academy Award for "Best Supporting Actress" for her performance.)

The Terrace's marble lobby and outdoor cafe were full of reporters, each looking for the scoop on the event. In the crush of people, the late Atlanta newspaper society editor, Yolande Gwin, mistook Vivien Leigh for just another reporter at a party for the *GWTW* stars.

In her book, *Yolande's Atlanta,* Gwin writes she was taken aback when this "stranger" asked to borrow her lipstick. "No!" Gwin replied. "That's just like my toothbrush; you can't have my lipstick." Finally Gwin relented, but only after the strange woman agreed to wipe it off with a tissue when she was finished.

Gwin did not realize who this "reporter" was until *GWTW* producer David Selznick walked into the Georgian Terrace Ballroom and called Vivien Leigh by name. Gwin later explained her actions, saying that Leigh just did not look like she did on the screen.[5]

THE BALL

A parade honoring *Gone With the Wind* moved up Peachtree Street on the afternoon of December 14. That evening, the *GWTW* ball was held at the Atlanta Municipal Auditorium (still standing and now part of Georgia State University). Margaret Mitchell did not attend the ball because it was sponsored by the Atlanta Junior League; she felt she had been snubbed by them some years before.

By a strange set of circumstances, the ball brought Georgian Terrace employee Monteen Haines and actress Olivia de Havilland together. In fact, Haines helped avert near disaster when de Havilland was left behind on the night of the Junior League Ball.

Miss de Havilland called Haines to her room on the ninth floor, where Haines helped the star with her makeup and dress. When Haines checked on the progress of the other celebrities, she discovered that the rest of the cast had already left. Haines made sure the hotel arranged for a car to rush the star to the party, but Miss de Havilland arrived late, just as she was being introduced to the crowd. The spotlight swept the boxes but was unable to find her. At the last moment, Laurence Olivier spotted Miss de Havilland and lifted the petite actress into the box, while she waved to the curious onlookers.[7]

A NIGHT TO REMEMBER

Loew's Grand Theatre recreated Tara's façade in front of its entrance for the premiere of the film on December 15, 1939. Most of the film stars attended, as did Margaret Mitchell and John Marsh. The sellout audience of 2,500 crowded inside, while thousands more stood outside.

The film was a resounding success. When the movie was over and thunderous applause subsided, Margaret Mitchell spoke, saying, ". . .Be kind to my Scarlett." The public was more than kind. *GWTW* set movie attendance and earnings records that stood for years. *Gone With the Wind* also won ten Academy Awards, including "Best Picture."

A TRAGIC DEATH

Margaret Mitchell lived—and died—on her beloved Peachtree Street. She spent her adolescent years living in her family's colonial-style mansion at 1401 Peachtree Street, and she met her untimely death just a few blocks south of there.

On the evening of August 11, 1949, Mitchell and her husband John Marsh decided to go see a show. The couple drove the short distance from their Ansley Park apartment and found a parking space across from the theater on the west side of Peachtree Street, just south of 13th Street.

As the couple began to cross the road, Hugh Dorsey Gravitt, an off-duty taxi driver, headed north on Peachtree in his private car. Witnesses estimated his speed at forty to fifty miles an hour. Marsh described what happened: "We had almost reached the center of the street when Gravitt's car came into view. From the first instant, I knew we were in danger."[8] John Marsh stepped forward, but his wife ran back to the curb, right into the path of the speeding car. She was hit at 8:20 P.M.

In addition to her head injuries, X-rays showed two fractures on her pelvis, but miraculously, no

internal injuries. Word of the accident spread quickly, and flowers and telegrams expressing concern flooded in. A special room had to be set up to handle the deluge of incoming telephone calls, which personal friends of Mitchell answered. Mitchell lived five days after the accident, never waking from her coma. On August 16, Mitchell's heart and lungs began to fail. She was pronounced dead at one minute before noon on August 16, 1949.

Today, Margaret Mitchell and John Marsh share the same headstone in an Oakland Cemetery plot. Mitchell's father Eugene and mother Maybelle are buried on the opposite side with double headstones. The square plot is adorned with a cedar tree planted in each corner, following an old tradition for marking Southern graves.

THE SHRINE

Hotel concierge staff members in Atlanta are often asked, "Where is Tara?" The answer to that question might surprise the visitor.

The O'Hara home cannot be viewed by any tourist, simply because it does not exist. Tara was a movie set, an antebellum façade created for the movie and dismantled after the film's completion. The movie set does still exist, however, and has made its way to Georgia, but its location is guarded as a precious secret by former Georgia first lady Betty Talmadge.

The movie façade returned to Georgia from Hollywood in 1959, and then languished in a barn in north Fulton County for almost twenty years after plans to turn it into a tourist attraction fell through. When the owner of the set, Julian Foster, was faced with the impending sale of the land where he kept the set stored, he began negotiations for the façade's sale. Ms. Talmadge indicated her interest in the set, but wanted to see firsthand its condition. Foster agreed to show her the materials, but he refused to allow an appraiser or lawyer to accompany them, claiming that he was the only living person who knew of the location, and he wanted to keep it that way until the deal was finalized. After a long and confusing drive through the countryside, Foster and Talmadge visited the set in its safe haven.

The original asking price of $375,000 had already dropped to $175,000, but the impending sale of the property forced Foster to take Talmadge's best offer. She offered $5,000, but only if a restoration architect decided the set could be restored. This arrangement was agreed upon, but when the time came for the architect to visit the site, Foster did not show up to take them to the secret barn. Talmadge began an investigation only to discover that Foster had died, taking the secret location of the barn with him!

No movie sets here!

Foster's widow still wanted to sell the set, but she had no idea where the barn was located. So Talmadge started driving, trying to remember all the twists and turns of her first visit to the barn. On the fourth day of searching, she found the barn.

Eventually the sale took place and the movie set was moved to another secret location. It will most likely remain in its second secret home until someone comes up with the estimated one million dollars to finance the museum-quality restoration.[8]

ATLANTA'S MONA LISA

A small Atlanta elementary school stands as a monument to
Atlanta's most famous author. Built in 1953, Margaret
Mitchell Elementary sits in a quiet residential neighborhood
at 2845 Margaret Mitchell Drive, N.W. The school houses
one treasure dear to any *Gone With the Wind* fan. Hanging
in the school auditorium is one of the most famous paintings
in the world: the oil portrait of Scarlett that appears in
GWTW. Patsy Wiggins, owner and curator of the Road to
Tara Museum remembers that the painting was first offered
to the High Museum. They rejected it because it "wasn't
art." The portrait was then given as a gift to the school.

7

T·H·E

DEVIL'S
FIREWIND
AND
OTHER
TRAGIC
TALES

The Devil's Firewind and Other Tragic Tales

PROUD FLESH

During the siege of Atlanta, not only were anesthetics to deaden pain unavailable, but effective medications were scarce. As a result, physicians generally relied on the "water treatment" as the chief medical procedure to heal injured soldiers.

This treatment involved wrapping wounds in thick layers of bandages, then soaking them continuously with cold water. In the case of an amputation, the cold water treatment was applied until all signs of inflammation disappeared and the wounded flesh (it was called "proud flesh") began to show signs of granulation or healing. One serious danger of the primitive treatment was gangrene, which sometimes developed if the cold, wet bandages were not removed soon enough.

Gangrene called for its own special treatment: the wounds were burned with nitric acid. John Will

Dyer, a private from Kentucky who was transported (on top of a box car) from Atlanta to a hospital in Newnan, helped administer this treatment. As he put it,

When pouring the acid on the "proud flesh" you would see smoke rise, the flesh sizzle and crisp up, and all this time the patient's screaming in agony. It took a stout heart and steady nerve to apply it. I hope never to have to do it again.

LITTLE MARY PHAGAN

Mary Phagan

In 1913, most Atlanta factory workers were white farmers who had come to the city to escape the sharecropping system. Family members, including children, had to help with the financial burdens of city life. Thirteen-year-old Mary Phagan was one of many child laborers working at the National Pencil Factory (at 39 Forsyth Street, between Alabama and Hunter Streets). On Saturday, April 26, 1913, Confederate Memorial Day, Mary stopped at the factory to pick up her wages. She was never seen alive again. In fact, Mary Phagan's lifeless body was found the next day in the factory basement by Newt Lee, the black night watchman.

The authorities quickly targeted two suspects: Lee, who found the body, and Leo Frank, Mary's superintendent, who claimed Mary picked up her money and left his office unaccosted. Frank, who was Jewish in a time and place notorious for its anti-Semitism, quickly became the target of the investigation. Two notes found at the scene, however, complicated matters;

Leo Frank

they pointed to Lee, the uneducated nightwatchman, as the murderer. The first note stated, "...that negro hire down here did this. i went to make water and he push me down that hole." The other note read, "He said her wood [sic] love me...but that long tall black negro did it buy his slef [sic]."[1]

Both Lee and Frank were questioned at the inquest, but the focus was on Frank and his moral turpitude. Georgia Epps, a friend of Mary's, testified that she was afraid of the factory superintendent because he had made familiar advances toward her. Then, rooming house proprietress, Nina Formby, testified that on the day of the murder Frank had tried to secure a room for himself and a young girl. Two days after the inquest ended, a policemen revealed that he had once apprehended Frank and a young girl in the woods. He later admitted he was mistaken about the incident, but Frank's guilt was as good as established already.

LITTLE MARY

Southerners viewed young girls as the epitome of purity and goodness; little Mary immediately became a martyr. She was buried in a white coffin to symbolize her innocence. Ten thousand mourners paid their respects at her funeral.

On the very day Frank was indicted for murder, Jim Conley (a short, black sweeper at the factory) admitted that he had written one of the murder notes. Conley was arrested, but because of the suspicions established concerning Frank, Conley's statement wasn't given much credence. Even when a factory foreman claimed to have seen Conley trying to wash blood out of his shirt, public attention stayed on Frank; in fact, the city's bacteriologist was never called to test the blood stains on Conley's shirt, and the grand jury never heard any of this information.

When the trial commenced, Conley testified against Frank. Conley swore that Frank was the murderer, and that Frank had asked him to write the two notes to place the blame on Lee. (Much to the defense counsel's surprise, Conley shocked the packed courtroom audience with the disclosure that Frank practiced oral sex. How he could have known this is still a mystery. Many believe that this one statement alone convicted Frank because of its "moral implications.")

Although Frank reportedly defended himself ably on the stand, the jury found him guilty and sentenced him to hang, a sentence that held through a series of appeals.

Governor John M. Slaton received a secret communication from Conley's lawyer claiming that Conley had confessed to the murder of Mary Phagan. Slaton also reexamined the evidence presented at the trial, and found Conley's testimony fraught with error. (One bizarre example: human feces was found at the bottom of the elevator shaft. While Conley admitted to defecating in the elevator shaft before the murder, he also swore in court that Frank had killed Mary upstairs in his office, then asked Conley to help him drag the body to the elevator to dispose of it in the basement. Slaton reasoned that if the elevator had been used at any time, the excrement, along with Mary's parasol and purse which were also in the shaft, would have been pulverized by the weight of the elevator. Therefore, the elevator could not have been used to transport the body and Conley's explanation could not be true.) Even though Slaton knew that his political career would be in jeopardy if he commuted Frank's death sentence to life imprisonment, he chose to do so, only one day before he was to leave the governor's office.

Frank went to prison, but his story did not end there. Two years after the murder, on August 16, 1915, twenty-five armed men, calling themselves the "Knights of Mary Phagan," arrived at the Milledgeville prison where Frank was being held. They cut prison telephone wires, detained the prison superintendent and warden in their homes, and overpowered guards. In less than ten minutes they had Leo Frank in their possession and were en route to Marietta.

The vigilantes tried to extract a confession from Frank, even promising Frank his freedom if he cooperated and admitted his guilt. Frank was allowed to speak on his own behalf; surprisingly, all but four of the vigilantes indicated their willingness to abandon the hanging after Frank's words. But with a posse hot on their trail and the prison far away, they decided to proceed with the lynching.

Early on the morning of April 17, Frank was hanged from a tree on Cobb County Sheriff W. J. Frey's land (an area now close to the Big Chicken in Marietta). The lynch mob chose this location so they could hang Frank as close to Mary Phagan's grave as possible.

The twenty-five men who lynched Frank were never apprehended. Many people, including the mayor of Atlanta, applauded the lynchmob's behavior.[2]

Almost seventy years after the deaths of Phagan and Frank, the *Nashville Tennessean* published a section featuring sworn statements of Alonzo Mann, a former Frank employee. Mann, who was a young boy in 1913, had testified in the Frank trial, but had withheld crucial information at his mother's urging. The *Tennessean* provided him with an opportunity to clear his conscience. He passed lie detector tests and testified to seeing Conley with Mary Phagan before her death. His assertions finally cleared Leo Frank's name.

Leo Frank was finally pardoned by the State of Georgia in 1986.

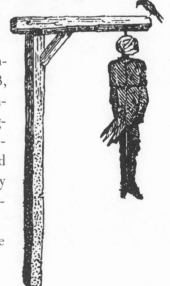

THE GREAT STONEHENGE EXPLOSION

Two Atlanta brothers, Sam and William Venable, were founding members of "The Knights of Mary Phagan" and were actively involved in the Ku Klux Klan. They bought Stone Mountain in 1887 and allowed the Klan to hold meetings on their land. (See chapter 3.) When his brother William died in 1905, Sam Venable used Stone Mountain granite to build an elaborate mansion he called "Stonehenge" at 1410 Ponce de Leon Avenue in Druid Hills. Although a bachelor, Venable built the nine-bedroom home to keep his family around him. The home, built in the early English Tudor style, resembled a fortress, and this was no accident. Venable was convinced a full-scale race war hovered on the horizon, and he wanted to be protected and prepared when it occurred.

Stonehenge, now part of St. John's Lutheran Church on Ponce de Leon Avenue.

Venable stocked the attic with ammunition and explosives (probably blasting materials from his Stone Mountain quarries). Unfortunately for him, one day a chimney overheated and set the roof on fire. The munitions ignited and the top of the house blew off. If the house had not been made of granite, it probably would have burned to the ground. As it was, the structural damage was easily repaired.

Venable died in 1939. Twenty years later, "Stonehenge" was sold to the congregation of St. John's Lutheran Church, the oldest Lutheran church in Atlanta. An octagonal sanctuary was added in 1969, also built with Stone Mountain granite. The church has kept many of the home's original features intact, including the carved mantelpiece and the steep vaulted ceilings.

THE DEVIL'S FIRE WIND

Fifty-three years after Sherman came from the North and blazed through Atlanta, a fire wind came from the South and engulfed seventy-three city blocks.

The first alarm came at 12:46 P.M. on Monday, May 21, 1917. Firefighters were called from as far away as Jacksonville, Florida, and Chattanooga, Tennessee. Unfortunately, the fire spread faster than the firefighters could contain it, and by 4:30 that afternoon, martial law was imposed.

The fire spread quickly from poor neighborhoods to the affluent area of Boulevard. Throughout Atlanta, streets were crowded with possessions hastily removed from burning houses. Rows of pianos lined one wealthy street; owners had placed them there hoping to save them from the fire.

In a controversial move, Mayor Asa Candler ordered the dynamiting of houses in the fire's path. Houses on Ponce de Leon and Boulevard were destroyed in an attempt to stop the raging conflagration. At 6:30 that evening the fire slowed; about thirty minutes later the winds reversed. The seventeen-hour fire stopped at Greenwood Avenue, between Ponce de Leon and Piedmont.

One thousand, nine hundred and thirty-eight houses, apartment buildings, shops, and churches were burned, leaving ten thousand people homeless. No one was killed by the fire, but two related deaths were reported: Ms. Bessie Hodges died of a heart attack as she watched her Boulevard house go up in smoke, and a young soldier was shot to death as he guarded against looters. The origin of the fire was never determined.

On the first anniversary of the fire, fourteen units of motorized fire vehicles arrived to replace the outdated horse-drawn fire-fighting equipment.

THE SECOND BATTLE OF ATLANTA

Atlanta already knew what it was like to have war waged in her own backyard. So during World War II, citizens diligently made preparations for a possible nighttime air raid by the enemy.

On Monday night, August 24, 1942, the Civil Defense scheduled a blackout to take place around ten o'clock. When the sirens sounded, citizens were ordered to turn out all lights (even their cigarettes), switch off their flashlights, and gather around the radio for instructions.

That drill may have seemed tame, but a more realistic one occurred the following month. At that time, airplanes dropped paper bag "bombs" (filled with flour) on the city below. One thousand firecracker-type "explosions" were set off to add to the sound effects.

If any citizen had trouble imagining what Atlanta might look like in the aftermath of war, the *Atlanta Journal* graphically illustrated it for its readers six months later. The February 19, 1942, headline read, "Death, Horror, and Destruction Could Smite Atlanta Any Day: Bombers from Hostile

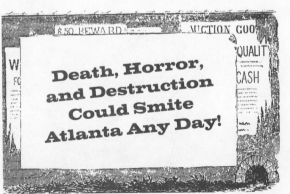

Carriers Might Easily Strike and Escape." The article was written to show what could happen if three squadrons of bombers attacked Atlanta. It was accompanied by pictures of bombed-out locations in London with captions like, "This Might Have Been On West Peachtree," "The Family Across the Street? They Might Have Done This to Georgia Tech." The railroad yards and Fort McPherson were among the areas targeted in the fictitious dawn attacks. The death toll of a future bombing was estimated in the hundreds, with many other victims likely trapped in the debris. Fortunately, none of these predictions ever came true.

THE TITANIC ON PEACHTREE STREET

The owners of the H.M.S. Titanic boasted "Not even God can sink her." The owners of the Winecoff Hotel, which still stands diagonally across from the Ritz-Carlton Hotel downtown, weren't quite so brazen; their advertisements only boasted of a fireproof luxury hotel. Because it was fireproof, the Winecoff had no fire escapes or sprinklers. It might be said that, like those involved with creating the Titanic, these visionaries were tempting fate.

The hotel was eighty percent full on the evening of December 6, 1946. The fire that devoured the hotel early in the morning of December 7 left 119 people dead and hundreds more injured. Evidence suggests that the fire was set by a disgruntled gambler. Current speculation holds that this gambler, unhappy with his losses from a floating crap game on the Winecoff's third floor, deviously started a fire on that floor which quickly spread to the higher levels.

Guests were caught off guard as the fire moved from the third floor up subsequent floors. Frantic to escape the fire and save themselves, people soaked

mattresses and stacked them against the doors to keep the flames out. Mothers dangled their children out of windows to protect them from the smoke, heat, and licking flames. Giving up on rescue, many mothers dropped their children to the pavement, hoping some onlooker would catch them.

Other hotel occupants tried to climb down to safety using makeshift sheet ropes. The lucky ones were able to reach a safety perch or a fireman. Others fell to their death. Those bodies immediately discerned as dead were not transported to Grady Hospital so that the injured living might get aid. Instead the dead were "laid out" neatly on the sidewalks and covered with any article of clothing that could be found. Grady's pathology department reported that the majority of victims sent to the hospital died from injuries suffered when they leapt from the windows or when they inhaled smoke and gases.

Four-year-old David Allen Patton III and his family were on an outing when they heard the news about the Winecoff fire. The radio unofficially reported that "hundreds of people were burned to death." Like so many Atlantans that morning, the family decided to forsake their outing and head toward the Winecoff to see if they could help. Atlanta also responded in record numbers to a call for donated blood.

"What I remember most," says Patton, "is the number of bodies laid out on the sidewalks with people walking around them as if they were 'mummies in a museum.'"

"I will never forget," Patton adds, "that the sun was shining as we headed outside the city limits; but as we returned toward town, the sun stopped shining. There was a cloud of smoke over the city that made it look dark, dismal, and foreboding. The city was mourning for the Winecoff dead. I remember that this dark cloud of sadness hung like a pall over the city for three days."[3]

The building *was* essentially fireproof; it still stands today. After the fire, it reopened as the Peachtree Hotel, then as a retirement home, but for most of the time it has been vacant, perhaps haunted by its tragic history.

TRAGEDY IN THE AIR

On June 3, 1962, 106 influential Atlantans boarded an Air France jet at Orly Airport. All were members of the Atlanta Art Association, returning from an art-buying expedition for the recently organized High Museum of Art. The Air France 707 roared down the runway, but something went wrong and the pilot tried to abort the takeoff. The wheels locked, the tires disintegrated, and the jet skidded off the end of the runway, sliding over 1200 feet into a field. The plane crashed into a small stone cottage and burst into flames. Only three people (flight attendants who were in the tail of the aircraft) survived the crash .

Out of this Orly tragedy came the Memorial Arts Center, now renamed the Robert W. Woodruff Arts Center. Over $13 million was raised through private donations to build an arts center around the High Museum in honor of those who had died. The French government donated a casting of Rodin's "L'Ombre," a melancholy statue whose head is set in perpetual mourning, to honor those lives lost in pursuit of art.

Rodin's "L'Ombre"

THE DUMP'S ON FIRE!

Mary Rose Taylor spearheaded efforts to restore the Windsor House Apartments where Margaret Mitchell wrote most of her novel *Gone With the Wind*. But at 4:26 A.M., September 17, 1994, Taylor's worst nightmare came true. "I dreamed I would get a call in the middle of the night, telling me the house was on fire. And today it came true."[4]

The fire, later determined to be arson, destroyed the roof and gutted the inside of the historic (circa 1899) three-story building. Even though all four walls were left standing, the south wall was badly damaged, with a large v-shaped gash from top to bottom. The building that Margaret Mitchell called "The Dump" was in ruins. "It's amazing it's even standing," said Taylor while surveying the damage.

"The Dump" two days after being gutted by fire on September 17, 1994.

Even though they had been raising money to restore the historic building, members of Margaret Mitchell House, Inc., did not actually own the house or the land on which it sits. Ironically, just two days before the fire, owner Childress Klein Properties rejected the group's most recent offer to buy the property. Margaret Mitchell House had planned a $2.6 million restoration project to turn the house into a museum in time for the 1996 Olympics.

But the story does have a happy ending: in 1994, the German corporation DaimlerBenz bought the land and house, vowing to restore "The Dump" before the 1996 Olympic Games.

8

★ T·H·E ★

GEORGIA
BILLYGOATS
➤ ➤ AND ◀ ◀
DOC
WALKER'S
FARM

The Georgia Billygoats and Doc Walker's Farm

WHAT A STEAL!

There *was* baseball before the Atlanta Braves. And they were champions!

The Gate City Club was made up of nine amateurs recruited from the ranks of the city's prominent young businesses. The Gate City nine challenged the city's first organized team, the Atlanta Baseball Club, to a game on May 18, 1866.

The Birth of BASEBALL

Baseball, spread by the Union armies during the Civil War, soon became popular all over the United States.

Atlantans started gathering at ten o'clock in the morning in anticipation of the 2:00 P.M. start time. The ballfield was located in a grove on Hunter Street, near Oakland Cemetery. Many of the wealthiest Atlantans arrived in their carriages; others walked the distance from downtown.

It was a batter's game, with twenty-five runs in the first inning. At one point, Gate City shortstop Robert Dohme was hit in the abdomen by a speeding fastball. He turned white and fell face down on the field. Ladies in the crowd fainted, and little children began to cry. In time Dohme revived, and the game continued. The final score:

The Atlanta Club	29
The Gate City Club	127

The Atlanta Club disbanded soon after their defeat.

Poor · LOSERS ·

The Gate City boys went on to play for the Amateur Championship of the Southern League. The home team was the Knoxville (Tennessee) Holstons, who were so certain of a win they planned a huge banquet after the game. The Gate City Club beat them by a close 21 to 19. The Holstons then called off the banquet and refused to speak to the team from Atlanta.

BRAVE NEW TEAM

The Atlanta Crackers were the next team to capture the city's interest. Organized in 1902, the team played in Piedmont Park for five years, then moved to what became its permanent home—Ponce de Leon Park, called "Old Poncey." A magnolia tree and a vine-covered embankment in the field's fair play territory made for some lively plays. However, nothing was as captivating as the activities that took place in the left field bleachers; this minor league team attracted major league gambling.

Baseball fans complained to officials that professional gamblers had set up shop in the stands, acting as bookies and ready to take bets on every pitch of the game. "They stand up with money in their hands and offer bets on whether the next pitch will be a ball or strike or anything else," said Solicitor General E. E. Andrews.[1] In response to these complaints, undercover police officers infiltrated the bleachers and began searching for lawbreakers.

For two nights, police detectives John Crankshaw and Glyn Cowan watched quietly as bets were made and money changed hands. The officers thought their cover had been blown the second night when the bookies suddenly sat down and stopped taking bets. "We thought they had gotten wise to us," the detectives told a reporter, "but we later found out that they had suffered a streak of bad luck in the fifth inning when an unusually large number of outfield flies almost exhausted their funds."

On the third night, August 21, 1946, Crankshaw and Cowan decided that they had collected enough evidence. In the third inning, uniformed officers moved into the stands and began arresting everyone the two detectives pointed out. The spectators quickly forgot about the game against the Chattanooga Lookouts; even the baseball players stopped and watched the field bleachers. Officers arrested a handful of the 300 to 400 gamblers in the stands that night. Thirteen men were hauled off to jail; the rest managed to slip into the packed stands before the law could reach them.

DOC WALKER'S FARM

Old Doc Walker was known not only for his medicinal abilities, but also for his green thumb. His 200-acre spread just north of town grew corn and cotton in abundance and housed a herd of cows. It eventually became home to the South's first college football game.

On February 20, 1892, the University of Georgia and Auburn University gathered on a field of honor at Doc Walker's farm to fight what was billed as the "Greatest Battle Known to College Athleticism." The players wore no helmets, and the referees wore cutaway jackets. It was a most civilized affair. Auburn won ten to zip, effectively trouncing the Georgia Billy Goats!

PIEDMONT PARK

Old Doc Walker's farm took the name Piedmont Park after the Piedmont Exposition in 1887.

Football suffered a setback in 1897 when Georgia's fullback Richard Von Gammon, eighteen, was dealt a fatal injury during a game. His death from a brain concussion triggered an outcry against football. Von Gammon's mother wrote the University of Georgia trustees asking them to continue the football tradition. The trustees and the public honored her wishes.

BUILD IT, AND THEY WILL COME

Atlanta Mayor Ivan Allen, Jr., once said that Atlanta Fulton County Stadium was planned "on land we didn't own, with money we didn't have, for a team we hadn't signed." Yet in 1964, city officials knew they had to have one thing before a major league baseball team would move to town. The city needed a first-class stadium.

In April, 1963, when the stadium was still in the "idea" phase, Kansas City Athletics owner Charlie Finley expressed interest in moving his team to Atlanta. Allen showed Finley possible stadium sites including what was once the Washington-Rawson neighborhood, located just southeast of the construction of the new I–75/ I–85 and I–20 interchange. Finley said if Atlanta built a stadium, his team would move there.

Mayor Allen quickly got the backing of Citizens and Southern National Bank and then convinced the city's business community that Atlanta was ready for a major league team. But when it came time to persuade the other major league owners, the city struck out. During the owner's meeting at the 1963 All-Star game in Cleveland, Ohio, the team owners refused to let Finley move his team.

During the discussions, however, something unexpected happened. Delbert Coleman, a major stockholder of the Milwaukee Braves, was impressed and promptly began negotiations with the group from Atlanta. A deal was struck, and construction for the new stadium began in February 1964—barely one year before the first scheduled Braves game was to be played in Atlanta.

Efforts to move the team hit a snag when major league team owners refused to let the Braves break their contract with Milwaukee. However, the Braves

were allowed to christen the new Atlanta stadium with an exhibition game against the Detroit Tigers. The city eventually hit a home run in negotiations, and the Braves officially moved to Atlanta in 1966, one year after the exhibition game.

To Ivan Allen, the stadium was more than a sporting arena; it established Atlanta as a major city. As he put it, "It [the Atlanta Braves] has changed our thinking, and the thinking of others around us. There's no provincial small town attitude here anymore. We're Big League!"[2]

ANOTHER STEAL!

When Ted Turner bought the Atlanta Braves in 1976, the team was stuck in the cellar of major league baseball. Fans often joked that the tickets couldn't even be given away.

In the very first year of Big Ted's ownership, fan attendance jumped by 300,000, even though the Braves' ranking still made them "cellar dwellers." It took fifteen years for the team to reach the status Ted Turner had envisioned. In the 1991 season the Braves climbed from "worst to first," rising like a phoenix from last place in the National League West to play in the World Series. That year, the Braves were involved in what was declared one of the greatest World Series in history. They fiercely battled the Minnesota Twins, but the Twins finally won the game and the series in the tenth inning of game seven. By 1995, when the Atlanta Braves clinched the World Series in their home stadium, the "cellar dweller" days seemed a distant memory. The "Loserville" title was a thing of the past, and another positive addition was made to Atlanta's self-image.

9

☆ ☆ T·H·E ☆ ☆
PHANTOM
O F   T H E
FOX,
☆ ☆ T·H·E ☆ ☆
DRIVE-UP
FUNERAL
MUSEUM,
➤➤ A N D ◄◄
OTHER
FACTS
➤➤ A N D ◄◄
FANCIES

•9•

The Phantom of the Fox, the Drive-up Funeral Museum, and Other Facts and Fancies

FOUR ROSES WHISKEY

It takes gumption to reference the government as proof of your whiskey's quality. But Rufus Rose did just that, printing "Ask the revenue officer" right on the label. In fact, Four Roses Whiskey was used as a medicinal whiskey because of its purity.

Rose established his distillery in Vinings, Georgia, just northwest of metro Atlanta, in 1867. As Rose's business grew, so did the Vinings community. Rose arranged for his distillery's tasting rooms to be open to the public, including women—whether accompanied

by a male companion or alone. (This was quite an unusual step for the time.) The Western and Atlantic Railroad began running excursion trains to the clear springs that provided the water for the whiskey, as well as to the distillery itself. Soon this daytrip became *the* thing to do for fashionable Atlantans.

Rose continued his Atlanta success with Four Roses Whiskey until 1909, when Georgia went dry. Rose then moved away to Tennessee, where he died in 1910.

His Atlanta mansion still stands at 537 Peachtree. Until recently, the mansion served as a museum with quite an eclectic collection. Not only could you see old Rufus Rose's homeplace, but also artifacts like: a model of Eli Whitney's first cotton gin, Margaret Mitchell's favorite watercolor painting, Edgar Allen Poe's silver gravy ladle, a Japanese Zero fighter, a 1955 Packard, and even Adolf Hitler's raincoat.

NUMBER, PLEASE

September 21, 1881, marks the date of the first telephone conversation in Atlanta. It was about noon, and workers had just finished installing a line connecting the Western and Atlantic freight depot with the train dispatcher's office in Union Station. Passenger agent B. W. Wrenn talked with Anton L. Kontz, another railroad employee; the exact conversation was as follows:

WRENN: "Who's there?"

KONTZ: "Alton Kontz. That's Wrenn, ain't it?"

WRENN: "Yes, I'm hungry. Send word to Henry Durand to get me a good dinner."[1]

Not exactly as cogent as telephone inventor Alexander Graham Bell's first words, but their conversation earned Wrenn and Kontz a place in Atlanta history.

By 1884, Southern Bell had its first long distance line—to Decatur. Young boys were hired to handle telephone switching duties, but in 1888 they were replaced by female operators. There were just too many complaints that the men were too excitable and used foul language.

The first dial telephones were installed in 1931. Southern Bell introduced direct long-distance dialing in 1957. By 1960, all-number calling was introduced.

ATLANTA'S ESTEEMED BRAIN TONIC AND INTELLECTUAL BEVERAGE

On November 25, 1885, prohibitionists won a referendum (by 228 votes) that barred liquor from Fulton County and Atlanta. Out of that movement for abstinence Coca-Cola was born.

Pharmacist John S. Pemberton was an early entrepreneur with an interest in niche marketing. Most of

THE FIRST SODA FOUNTAIN

Aaron Alexanders opened Atlanta's first soda fountain establishment with ice in 1850.

his inventions started in his brass kettle out in the backyard at 107 Marietta Street (near CNN Center today). Here he created "Lemon and Orange Elixir," "Globe Flower Cough Syrup," and "Dr. Pemberton's Indian Queen Magic Hair Dye." But Pemberton was worried about Prohibition's effect on his latest invention, a drink called "French Wine Cola," until he came upon a wonderful solution—he would market his invention as a "soft drink" to help cure headaches.

Early Coke · COMPETITION ·

Cocaine was common in drinks at the turn of the century. Other "soft beverages" containing cocaine included "Cola Coke," "Wise Ola," "Rocco-Cola," and the Rainbow Bottling Company's "Dope."

In his formula for French Wine Cola, Pemberton took advantage of the growing interest in the kola nut. Since Prohibition denied the use of alcohol for "medicinal purposes," alternative treatments became substantially more important. The kola nut was one of the more popular substitutions. The alcoholic extract from coca leaves, called coca wine, had been introduced in America and Europe in the 1860s, and at the time, cost five dollars an ounce. This cocaine derivative was widely used and was believed to fight depression, to conserve energy, and

to serve as an "unequivocal aphrodisiac." In fact, Thomas Edison loved Vin Mariani, a French wine laced with cocaine. Pope Leo XIII negotiated a discount with the manufacturer and distributor, and all clergy got a ten percent discount on their purchase of cocaine. U. S. Grant took cocaine to ease his throat cancer while he was writing his memoirs.

Pemberton took the flavor of the kola nut extract and combined it with a few other ingredients, creating a syrup he marketed as a "brain tonic." Syrup in hand, Pemberton strolled to Jacob's Pharmacy (at the corner of Peachtree and Marietta) for a taste test. He instructed the pharmacist's assistant Venable to mix the caramel-colored syrup with water and chill it with ice. The first taster pronounced the mixture "delicious." And so the brain tonic was born.

A mistake turned Pemberton's creation from medicine to fountain drink. Venable accidentally mixed the elixir with carbonated water, which made the drink even more delicious. Suddenly it could compete with ginger ale and root beer, which, like flavored soda water, had been around for years. The drink was named "Coca-Cola" after the coca leaves and cola nuts it contained. Frank Robinson, Pemberton's bookkeeper, scripted the now famous Coca-Cola logo. (Robinson was chosen because of his excellent penmanship.) The first year, Pemberton sold twenty-five gallons of his syrup. He took in fifty dollars and spent $73.26 on advertising.

Two years later, Asa Candler, a proprietor of the drug store where Pemberton bought his supplies, offered to buy out Pemberton. The inventor accepted and sold Candler a two-thirds interest for $1200.

Pemberton sold the remaining interest for $500. Candler gave most of his share in the Coca-Cola business to his family, who sold the rights to the product. In 1919, a group led by Ernest Woodruff and Samuel Dobbs paid $25 million for what would become a billion-dollar drink.

The original Coca-Cola mixture contained five milligrams of cocaine per drink. But in 1903, the Atlanta City Council passed an ordinance prohibiting the sale of cocaine at soda fountains. By 1910, cocaine was considered America's new vice.

While the Coca-Cola Company freely admits that cocaine was once one of its drink ingredients, there are other ingredients which are still well-kept secrets. These components are referred to as "7X." It is rumored that only three people know the mystery ingredients, and for security reasons these three never fly together.

FROM RAGS TO RICH'S

The story of Rich's began in 1867, when nineteen-year-old Hungarian immigrant Morris Rich borrowed $500 from his brother William to open a dry goods business. The store at 36 Whitehall Street was modest, but it attracted many customers who sought to rebuild after the Civil War. For those who could not afford to pay cash, Rich bartered for whatever his customer could offer: usually chickens, eggs, or corn. By 1924 Rich's had grown to seventy-five departments with over 800 employees and had relocated downtown to 45 Broad Street.

As the store grew, so did its generosity. For instance, during World War I, when the price of cotton plummeted because farmers could not get their crop to overseas markets, Rich's purchased numerous bales of cotton to help support the farmers. When another cotton crisis occurred in 1931, the store accepted "cotton for cash." During the depression in the 1930s, when the city of Atlanta could not afford to pay its school teachers, instructors received certificates called scrip. Rich's allowed teachers to turn in the scrip in exchange for cash. And in 1945, when the United States Army's time-locked safe would not open in time to pay troops, Rich's advanced the payroll for Fort McPherson soldiers going on weekend leave.

Shut the
· WINDOWS ·

Believe it or not, one major innovation for Atlanta's hometown store was prompted by the trains' dirt and smoke. Rich's sat very close to the downtown train tracks and suffered through the worst of the noise and smoke. In 1926, Rich's installed an indoor cooling system, which allowed it to close its windows and protect its customers and merchandise from the ill effects of the trains. In so doing, Rich's became the first department store in the country to be completely air-conditioned. Rich's did not make a big deal about their modernization, however; store executives were not sure the air-conditioning would work, and they didn't want to call attention to the innovation in case the system failed.

Unfortunately, the big downtown Rich's department store is no longer around; it closed its doors for good in 1990. At seven-thirty in the morning on June 5, 1994, 850 pounds and 1,200 charges of explosives were set off, causing

Rich's Store for Homes to implode and collapse upon itself. One hundred and thirty thousand tons of rubble were left behind.

During the few weeks between demolition and the start of construction on a new structure, archae-

ologists were allowed to conduct a dig to see if they could unearth any relics from old Atlanta. Prior to the construction of the Rich's Store for Homes in 1945–46, the downtown Atlanta block had housed resi-dences, cotton warehouses, mule stables, saloons, and the infamous National Pencil Company where thirteen-year-old Mary Phagan was murdered. The artifacts found dur-ing the dig included a Confederate uniform button, kitchen utensils, jewelry, and an unexploded twelve-pound shell left over from the Battle of Atlanta.

"Meet me at Rich's clock!" The clock at the corner of Broad and Alabama Streets served as a convenient meeting place. It is one of the few remaining pieces from Rich's original downtown building.

THE DRIVE-UP FUNERAL MUSEUM

The Atlanta area's Antique Funeral Museum at Pope Dickson & Son Funeral Home in Jonesboro may be the only drive-up funeral museum in the world. Memento moris, morbid souvenirs of our funereal past, are displayed in the two large picture windows of the museum. The centerpiece of the mortuary sci-ence exhibit is the horse-drawn hearse used to carry Alexander Hamilton Stephens's body from the Geor-gia governor's mansion on Peachtree Street to its fi-nal resting place in Crawfordville, Georgia. A "cool-ing board," a flat board used to prepare the body inside the deceased's own home, is also on display.

The portable cooling board, which folds up in its own carrying case, was used for the embalming of the body. Then the board was covered and the corpse laid out for display until burial. (Tradition dictated that the body could not be placed in its casket until the day of the funeral.) Flower arrangements—painted black, as was the custom—are also exhibited.

WHERE DID MORTICIANS COME FROM?

Embalming became an art during the Civil War. Preparing the bodies for travel from the battlefield also created a new occupation: the mortician. With the necessary increase in funeral directors, there also came an unprecedented economic and aesthetic need for coffins. Following the laws of supply and demand, the Gate City Coffin Company set up shop, employing over eighty employees and creating 20,000 coffins per year.

1895 ATLANTA COTTON STATES AND INTERNATIONAL EXPOSITION

The 1895 Atlanta Cotton States and International Exposition (the Cotton Exposition for short) was a hundred-day World's Fair. In the fall of 1895, over one million people came to Atlanta to see the agricultural extravaganza, which, with its more than 6,000 exhibits and fifty magnificent buildings, was the most spectacular show on earth. Over 25,000 people marched through the front gates, accompanied by military bands playing Victor Herbert's newest march, "Salute to Atlanta." John Phillip Sousa wrote "King Cotton" for the exposition. This event was one of the highlights of the century.

The Exposition featured camel rides, the world's tallest ferris wheel, boat rides on Lake Clara Meer, and "shooting the chute" in little rail cars which plunged into the lake. Lake Clara Meer was between the Wild West Show, the midway, and the "ovoid," an egg-shaped main exhibition area.

Exhibits included the Women's Building, with important displays by and about women. Forty women managers were behind the creation of this building, which was also designed by a female architect, Elise Mercur of Pittsburgh. The response from women visitors was so great that another building became necessary; this annex contained inventions by women, along with displays explaining advances made by women in the arts, sciences, and entertainment field.

Another popular exhibit was the Negro Building, the first exhibit at any World's Fair devoted to the life, character, and work of the African-American race.

While agricultural in theme, the Exposition was provocative in scope. For example, attendees could see Nellie White, "Trilby of the Midway," dance in flesh-colored tights with a trio of "hoochie-coochie" dancers in exotic costumes. (One dancer created quite a scandal when she flaunted a cigarette in public.) The moving picture show, however, did not create much of a stir with visitors; it was canceled due to lack of interest.

The Atlanta Exposition began to transform the national perception of Atlanta from that of a Southern town to that of an upscale cosmopolitan city.

An advertisement for the Atlanta Exposition of 1881.

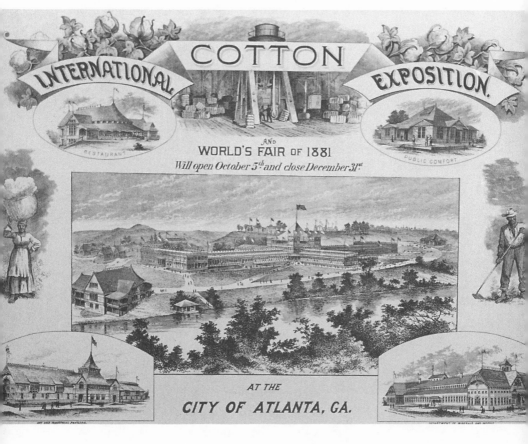

THE LITTLE ZOO THAT GREW

Atlanta's zoo began as an afterthought. Wealthy lumber man George V. Gress bought a bankrupt circus for $4,435 in 1889, kept the rail cars and wagons, and donated the animals to the city of Atlanta. Atlanta gained an instant zoo: one hyena, two African lionesses, two silver lions, one black bear, two wildcats, one jaguar, one gazelle, a raccoon, an elk, a Mexican hog, two deer, a camel, two monkeys, and two serpents. One hundred acres of Grant Park became home to the new zoo, christened the "Grant Park Zoo."

In 1935, when one of Asa Candler Sr.'s baboons escaped from his private collection of exotic animals and terrorized the woman next door, it became clear that his animals needed a more appropriate home. Asa Candler, Jr., donated his father's private collection of exotic animals to the city, increasing both the number and the variety of animals in Grant Park Zoo's collection.

THE NEW ZOO

In February, 1984, a Humane Society of the United States survey confirmed what many already believed: Atlanta's Zoo stank, both literally and figuratively. The Grant Park Zoo was named one of the ten worst zoos in the country. The report's findings included the following atrocities:

- The mud and feces were so deep in the white-tailed deer exhibit that the animals could barely walk.
- A Kodiak bear was trapped at the bottom of a dry moat, so zoo employees just threw food to her regularly.

- A thirteen-year-old elephant named "Twinkles" disappeared from the zoo and turned up dead in a traveling circus. The circus owner said the ailing elephant was given to him by the zoo, and she died thirty hours after the pachyderm was in his possession. The remaining elephants at the zoo mourned Twinkles—one grieving elephant beat on Twinkles's door over and over with his trunk.
- Prairie dog holes were filled with concrete while the creatures were asleep in their dormant winter phase. Miraculously, nine dogs survived.
- A Parks and Recreation worker admitted he had been buying rabbits, pigs, and ducks from the zoo to slaughter and serve at his dinner table.[2]

Ironically, this stinging report was the beginning of better times for the struggling zoo. The publicity surrounding the facility's loss of accreditation eventually led to its revitalization and transformation into a world-class zoo. Today's facility, renamed Zoo Atlanta, is respected and recognized nationwide.

WILLIE B., ONE AND TWO

The gorilla named Willie B. who makes his home in Zoo Atlanta today is *not* the original Willie B. After Grant Park Zoo's $400,000 primate house opened in 1959, a baby gorilla named Willie B. moved in. The primate became so popular, he drew 663 votes in the 1960 race for 5th District Congressman. (Although Willie B. lost the election, he did finish ahead of two human candidates!) The entire city mourned when the little gorilla died unexpectedly in 1961.

WILLIE B. IN OFFICE

Both Willie B.'s were named after former Atlanta Mayor William B. Hartsfield.

Today's Willie B. is Willie B. the Second. Willie B. II came to Atlanta as a baby from the rain forests of Africa. He lived alone for twenty-seven years, until Zoo Atlanta's natural habitat, the Ford African Rain Forest, opened in 1988. Willie B. left his cage to join a group of other gorillas in the outdoor habitat, and soon fathered Kudzoo, his first offspring.

IVAN

The efforts to assimilate Willie B. into a natural setting were so successful that Atlanta's zoo was also deemed to be the best home for Ivan, a gorilla who had spent most of his life on display in a shopping center.

During Ivan's early years, he was raised like a human child. He wore children's clothing and in the 1960s was taken by his Tacoma, Washington, owners to the local drive-in restaurant. When Ivan's strength became a concern, he was moved to a cage and became the showpiece of the "World Famous B & I Circus Store" in a Tacoma shopping center. After the center filed for bankruptcy, a judge ordered that Ivan be moved to a zoo.

On October 12, 1994, Ivan arrived at his new home at Zoo Atlanta.

Another · NAMESAKE ·

One condition of Ivan's move to Atlanta was that the zoo never change his name. As it turns out, "Ivan" couldn't be a more appropriate name for a Zoo Atlanta primate. The mayor who succeeded Willie B.'s namesake, William B. Hartsfield, was an Ivan—Ivan Allen, Jr.

VOICES FROM BEYOND

RALLY OF THE DEAD

Where there is a graveyard, there *will* be talk of ghosts, and Atlanta's Oakland Cemetery, where hundreds of Atlanta's dead sleep, is no exception. The spooky rumors surrounding the city's oldest graveyard describe "The Rally of the Dead," a roll call of ghostly voices accompanied by the beat of a phantom drum that seems to emanate from the Confederate section of the cemetery.

Patrolman Roy O. Eddleman worked the cemetery's midnight-to-dawn shift for several months during the late 1920s. He dismissed the ghost stories as foolishness until the dead made their presence known to him during his watch. When Eddleman heard the "Rally" for himself, he quickly became a believer. As he explained, "Nobody could have mistaken it. It had a definite, expert rhythm like a snare drum played very far away. Although I investigated the noise, I was never able to find out what caused it. I would hear confused sounds coming from the Confederate section. The general effect was that of a number of people moving around and calling to each other. What caused it? Don't ask me."[3]

UNKNOWN SOLDIERS

It is unfortunate that no one wrote down the names spoken aloud in that spectral roll call years ago, since the several hundred unknown Confederate soldiers who lie in Oakland's unmarked graves will remain anonymous for all eternity.

THE PHANTOM OF THE FOX

In 1929, the Fox Theatre introduced the first self-operating push-button elevator to Atlanta. It is still working today, but seemingly with a mind of its own. Legend has it that a phantom elevator operator sometimes takes over the controls. No matter what floor is selected, the elevator often heads straight to the seventh floor and stops as if waiting for someone to come aboard.

The "ghost" is thought to be the spirit of a mistress who once had a private suite on the seventh floor. To this day, backstage workers at the Fox report hearing mysterious creaks, groans, sighs, and whispers. Walk through the Egyptian Ballroom at night, and the sounds of "ghost footsteps" may follow your stride across the floor. (While researching this book, the authors were given a tour of the Fox by general manager Edgar Neiss. To everyone's surprise the elevator first stopped on the seventh floor so the ghost could tour with us.)

THE WOMAN IN SILVER

One of Atlanta's most enduring stories is the ghostly tale of the woman in silver. On October 31, 1941, a young couple returning home from a Halloween party in College Park reported seeing a beautiful young woman sitting on the curb near the railroad bridge at Stewart and Dill Avenues. It was about two o'clock in the morning, and the woman, shimmering through the rain in a silvery evening gown, was crying pitifully.

The couple pulled over and offered her a lift. She accepted and climbed into the back seat of the couple's two-door sedan. The young lady gave them a Peachtree Street address, but continued her sobbing, not uttering another word during the drive across town.

"Well, here we are," said the driver as he pulled the car up to the house. "Would you like me to go to the door with you?" Hearing no reply, he looked back and the girl in the shimmering dress was gone! She had vanished!

Seeing a light on in the old colonial-style house, the couple walked to the door and rang the bell. An elderly woman answered and the confused couple explained what had happened. They described what the young woman looked like, that she had long black curls, and was wearing a flowing, silvery dress.

"That," said the old lady, "was my daughter. You are the fourth couple who has brought her home tonight. You see, she was killed in an automobile accident on Stewart Avenue fourteen years ago tonight."[4]

Rumor has it that the woman in silver still appears every Halloween, even though her home on Peachtree Street no longer exists.

HENRY'S HAUNT

Henry Heinz had everything a man could want in the Atlanta of 1943. He lived in a beautiful Mediterranean-style mansion at 1610 Ponce de Leon Avenue, was married to Lucy Candler, the only daughter of Coca-Cola founder Asa Candler, and was prosperous in his own right as vice president of the C&S Bank. But Heinz, like many other residents of that era in Druid Hills, was worried about a recent rash of burglaries in the well-to-do neighborhood. His home had already been robbed twice, so Heinz bought several guns and began target practice to prepare for the next burglar's strike.

A burglar did find his way to the Heinz residence on the night of September 29, 1943. Heinz yelled upstairs to his wife, telling her he heard an intruder in the house and urging her to hurry downstairs with his gun. As Lucy Candler Heinz headed down the steps, without the gun, she heard her husband's cry and then two gunshots.

Mrs. Heinz hurried to the library and saw her husband struggling with another man. She ran into the next room to get a gun. When she returned, the intruder was gone and her husband was mortally wounded. Emergency number 911 did not exist then, so Lucy called Grady Hospital directly, then the police and her son-in-law, Dr. Bryant Vann.

Vann and the police arrived at the same time, and, mistaking each other for intruders, opened fire. The officers were not injured, but Dr. Vann was shot in the chest and right wrist and was beaten with the butts of the officers' guns until the misunderstanding was explained.

Despite the confusion of the gun battle, the police retrieved two clues that pointed to the identity of the murderer: a perfect set of fingerprints and the inner workings of a broken wrist watch.

A year and four months after the murder, police arrested Horace Blalock, a burglar captured after breaking into the home of Atlanta lawyer Hughes Spalding. Blalock's fingerprints matched those at the Heinz estate, and a jeweler reported that Heinz had indeed brought in a broken watch for repair two weeks after the Heinz murder.

Blalock confessed to the murder, admitting he had also broken into the Heinz estate two previous times. Although he made $200 each month with the railroad, he burglarized homes to support his penchant for a lottery game known as "The Bug." Blalock was convicted of murder and sentenced to life in

prison. He served ten years before being paroled.

Mrs. Heinz moved out of the estate right after the murder, and the home was converted into apartments. Tenants reported hearing unusual sounds in the middle of the night, and many residents became convinced the ghost of Henry Heinz walked the grounds. The reports described footsteps on the lawn of the estate, then what sounded like gunshots. The tenants gradually moved out, and the estate deteriorated and became overgrown with weeds. For years, the eerie, rundown appearance of the house itself contributed to its ghostly reputation. In the 1980s, the white-stuccoed mansion was painted pink and converted into the Lullwater Estate condominiums.

THE PINK FACTOR

Henry Heinz has not been seen (or heard) haunting his former home since it was painted pink!

THE GUARDIAN ANGEL AND
A BOUQUET OF JONQUILS

One of the most haunting images of Margaret Mitchell's last days was captured in a picture taken outside her hospital door. Lorene Moore, a nurse at Grady Hospital, was standing watch in the outside hallway to keep the press and curious fans from disturbing the author. *Atlanta Constitution* photographer Ryan Sanders snapped a picture of Moore, and captured on film something unusual—a shadowy image

behind the nurse, next to the doorway. Sanders had seen no one there and could not recall doing anything during the photo development that would create such an effect.

"I let it go by just thinking of the picture as the 'Guardian Angel,'" said Ryan.[5] The day after the picture was taken, Margaret Mitchell died.

There have been other shadowy sightings associated with the *Gone With the Wind* author; one is specifically called the "Ghost of Margaret Mitchell."

A few years before her book was a huge success, Mitchell bought the Lemuel P. Grant mansion in partnership with Boyd Eugene Taylor, an *Atlanta Journal-Constitution* writer. The Mitchells had planned to restore the Italianate home to its former glory.

In 1978, Taylor told the *Atlanta Journal Magazine:* "I know no one will believe that she really comes here now, but she does—every spring. I can only tell you what I see, and I can only tell you not to be afraid of ghosts. Margaret just wanders through the house, looking things over. She never talks, and she always carries jonquils. The first night she came I was very shocked. I went out to her grave at Oakland Cemetery the next day. I'd never been there before. But I was almost certain of what I'd find. The plot is covered by a bed of jonquils."

TWINKLE, TWINKLE LITTLE STAR

Since the Fox Theatre opened in 1929, audiences there have stared upward to watch the stars twinkle and clouds slowly meander across the sky. The weather inside is almost always cool and partly cloudy, with a sky just dark enough for the twinkling stars to shine through. The outdoor sky in an indoor building was ahead of its time when it was built, and continues to be an attraction today.

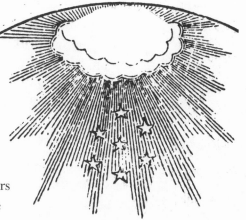

The effect of twinkling stars was created by painting the vaulted ceiling azure blue, then sprinkling it with ninety-six two-inch crystals illuminated with miniature eleven-watt bulbs. The result is a soft, twinkling light.

The cloud's movement is more complicated. A "Junior Brenograph" projects the lazily floating clouds that move across the sky. The clouds are set on a circular disk, timed to make a complete revolution every hour and forty-five minutes. The "Master Brenograph" can also project other weather conditions, such as snow, rain, and fog. Perhaps the most popular effect is the appearance of sunrise in the eastern part of the Fox auditorium, which then shifts to the noonday sun, and then to a flaming sunset over the right-hand side of the proscenium curtain.

AIN'T WE GOT FUN!

"It's the greatest thing since the opening of *Gone With the Wind*," exclaimed Atlanta Mayor Maynard Jackson on the evening the World of Sid and Marty Krofft opened.

Billed as the world's largest indoor amusement park, the $14 million attraction opened at the top of the Omni International complex on May 26, 1976. Ambitious city leaders hoped the park would help revitalize Atlanta's downtown and lure tourists and prosperity to the inner city.

But only 300,000 visitors showed up that first summer and fall, far short of the 940,000 visitors needed to show a profit. Customers complained the rides often broke down or were too tame. Visitors were fascinated by the sixty-ton Crystal Mythology Carousel—when it worked. Businesses and restaurants inside the Omni complex complained about the noise coming from the park. No efforts seemed to alleviate the problem.

The park closed without advance notice on November 7, 1976, less than six months after the first visitors rode up the park's 205-foot escalator—at the time the longest in the world. Remnants of the park remained on the Omni's eighth floor for years, and were visible from the courtyard below. The area was finally sealed off when Ted Turner bought Omni International and turned it into CNN Center, home for the Cable News Network.[6]

AFTERWORD

"But Atlanta was of [Scarlett's] own generation, crude with the crudities of youth and as headstrong and impetuous as herself....Scarlett had always liked Atlanta for the very same reasons that made Savannah, Augusta and Macon condemn it. Like herself, the town was a mixture of the old and new in Georgia, in which the old often came off second best in its conflicts with the self-willed and vigorous new town that was born—or at least christened—the same year she was christened."

—*Gone With the Wind*, Margaret Mitchell

There are many good reasons Atlanta often identifies so closely with Margaret Mitchell's *Gone With the Wind,* several of which are explained in this passage. Atlanta has never been a bastion of the "Old South" in the sense that Charleston and Savannah have been, and has never sought to be.

When the Civil War destroyed all of the physical and psychological foundations the new city had established, Atlanta was forced into resurrection and regeneration from the ashes of her past. From that point on, Atlanta has looked to the future, and has become a center for change, innovation, and action, as well as a common destination for people from every other corner of the country and the world.

Henry W. Grady called this new reality "The New South," a state of mind and place that builds on history without repeating it and that embraces new inhabitants with open arms. Each of the questions that inspired this book reveals a part of Atlanta's own special story, with its own characters, context, and meaning. These questions help us see Atlanta as a character in her own right, a place with a rich past, a unique point of view, and an unforgettable personality.

We hope you have enjoyed this journey into Atlanta's checkered, always interesting past, and have come to admire the city that she has been, as well as the city she is becoming.

NOTES

Chapter 1

1. J. W. Mason, "Atlanta's Matronymic." Unpublished manuscript. 158/DU–28–15, Speeches & Articles, Box 1, File 2, Atlanta History Center, Atlanta, Georgia.
2. E. M. Mitchell, Letter to J. L. Edgerton, Western Newspaper Union, Manuscript 158/DU–28–14, Box 1, File 1, 1894–1928, Atlanta History Center, Atlanta, Georgia.
3. J. Schonbak, "The Hawking Hucksters of Humbug Square," *Business Atlanta* (April 1985): 130–132.

Chapter 2

1. J. R. Hornady, *Atlanta Yesterday, Today, and Tomorrow*, (American Cities Book Company, 1922), 38.
2. B. McCullar, *This Is Your Georgia* (Montgomery, AL: Viewpoint Publications, 1972), 481.
3. S. W. McCallie, "An Atlanta Quiz," *Atlanta Constitution Sunday Magazine and Feature Section* (26 May 1940): 4.
4. Ibid.

Chapter 3

1. R. L. Radford, *Prelude to Fame, Crawford Long's Discovery of Anaesthesia* [sic] (Los Altos, CA: Geron-X, Inc., 1969).
2. B. McCullar, *This Is Your Georgia,* 474.
3. Herndon Family Papers, Herndon House, Atlanta, Georgia.
4. E. M. Mitchell, Manuscript 158/DU–28–14, Box 1, File 1, 1894–1928, Atlanta History Center, Atlanta, Georgia.
5. Glenna Mae Davis, personal interview.
6. Hank Aaron, News Conference, Atlanta: WXIA-TV, 13 April 1994.

Chapter 4

1. "Divorces Exceed Marriages, Jury Bares in Report," 1.
2. Celestine Sibley, "Two Governors" (Series), *Atlanta Constitution* (3 July 1974): 3B.
3. H. Martin, *Atlanta and Environs III* (Athens, Georgia; University of Georgia Press, 1987), 325–328.

Chapter 5

1. A. W. King, "Evolution of the Wheel or Perils of Early Bicycling in Atlanta," *Atlanta Historical Bulletin*, VIII (December 1947): 1.
2. Glenna Mae Davis, personal interview.

Chapter 6

1. D. Hall, 292–294.
2. M. Walker, *Margaret Mitchell and John Marsh: The Love Story Behind Gone With the Wind* (Atlanta: Peachtree Publishers, 1993), p. 197, referenced to R. Harwell, *"Gone With the Wind" as Book and Film,* 59.
3. Ibid., 198, referenced to H. Latham, "How I Found *Gone With the Wind*," *Atlanta Journal Magazine*, n.d., 20–22.
4. Cosmic Muffin Inc.; America Online: Acmeanswer.
5. Yolande Gwin, *Yolande's Atlanta* (Atlanta, Georgia: Peachtree Publishers, 1983), 27.
6. Walker, *Mitchell and Marsh*, p. 96.
7. M. Haines, personal interview.
8. B. Talmadge, personal interview.

Chapter 7

1. L. Dinnerstein, *The Leo Frank Case* (Athens, Georgia: The University of Georgia Press, 1987), 3.
2. Ibid., 129.
3. David Allen Patton, personal interview.
4. Mary Rose Taylor, personal interview.

Chapter 8

1. "Police Raid Ponce de Leon Bleachers," *Atlanta Constitution* (22 August 1946): 1.
2. *Fan*, Braves 1977 Scorebook, 9, 36.

Chapter 9

1. F. Garrett, *Atlanta and Environs, II*, (Athens, Georgia: University of Georgia Press, 1987), 23–24.
2. S. Faludi, *Atlanta Constitution*, 4 June, 13 June, 19 August 1984.
3. M. Steedman, "Ghost in a Fruit Jar," *Atlanta Journal Magazine* (20 June 1937): 11.
4. R. Hudspeth, "Beware If You See This Girl on Halloween," *Atlanta Journal* (31 October 1981): 1B.
5. "Photo Showed Guardian Angel at Margaret Mitchell's Doorway," *Atlanta Constitution,* 16 June 1960.
6. P. Troop and T. Walker, "Krofft World Park Closed by Owners," *Atlanta Journal* (12 March 1976): 24A.

Aaron, H. News Conference. Atlanta: WXIA-TV, 13 April 1994.

Aaron, H., and Wheeler, L. *I Had a Hammer*. New York: HarperCollins Publishers, 1991.

"Act of Providence: Visit Saves Girl Delegate from Tragedy." *Atlanta Journal*, 9 December 1946, 3.

"Atlanta—A City of the Modern South." *Atlanta Journal Magazine,* 12 July 1942, 6.

"Atlanta's Finest Haunts." *Atlanta Magazine*, October 1993, 17.

Auchmutey, J., and Donosky, L., eds. *True South*. Atlanta: Longstreet Press, 1994.

Bell, P. "The Ether Controversy." Manuscript No. 59, Box 1, Folder 20, Atlanta History Center.

Bibb, P. *It Ain't as Easy as It Looks*. New York: Crown Publishers, 1993.

Blair, R. "Do You Know Atlanta?" *Atlanta Constitution Sunday Magazine and Feature Section*, 26 May 1940,
    4.

Blew, M. "Winecoff's Holocaust Burned Tragic Gaps in Youth Assembly." *Atlanta Journal,* 8 December
    1946, 10A.

Botkin, B. (Ed.). *A Treasury of Southern Folklore*. New York: American Legacy Press, 1949.

Boyd, K. W. *The Historical Markers of North Georgia*. Atlanta: Cherokee Publishing Company, 1993.

Brown, M. "Passports to Travel in Georgia." *Atlanta Journal Magazine*, 14 August 1940, 7.

Bryans, R. "Let's Cry In Silence" (Series). *Atlanta Journal*, 1 July 1974, 1+; 2 July 1974, 1; 5 July
    1974, 1.

"Choose Money Over History." *Atlanta Constitution*, 19 September 1990, 9A.

Confield, R. "Ghostly Past." *Peachtree*, May 1994, 8: 15–19.

Crutchfield, J.A. (Ed.) *The Georgia Almanac and Book of Facts*. Nashville, TN: Rutledge Hill Press, 1986.

"Dangling Sheet-ropes Tell Gruesome Story." *Atlanta Journal*, 8 December 1946, 10A.

Davis, G.M. Personal interview, 29 May 1994.

Davis, E. Personal interview, 29 May 1994.

Dinnerstein, L. *The Leo Frank Case*. Athens, GA. The University of Georgia, 1987.

"Disputed Territories: *Gone With the Wind* and Southern Myths," exhibit at Atlanta History Center, 5
    May–31 October 1994.

"The Eternal Flame." Atlanta History Folder. Atlanta: Georgia Archives Building.

Evans, E. *Judah P. Benjamin*. New York: The Free Press, 1988.

Fan, Braves 1977 Scorebook, 9, 36.

Faludi, S. "A Distressing Day at Zoo Atlanta." *Atlanta Constitution*, 4 June 1984, 1E.

————. "Circus Owner Explains How Twinkles Died." *Atlanta Constitution*, 19 August 1984, 3B.

————. "Worker Says He Bought Rabbits from the Zoo to Eat." *Atlanta Constitution*, 13 June 1984, 1.

Foskett, K., and Kelly, M. L. "After the Smoke Clears McGriff Fires Up Braves." *Atlanta Constitution*,
    21 July 1993, 1A+.

Flexner, S. B. *Listening to America*. New York: Simon & Schuster, 1992.

Foster, D. C. "Gate City of the South, Farewell!" *Business Atlanta,* May 1987, 62–70.

"Four Children See Santa, Then Perish." *Atlanta Journal,* 9 December 1946, 2.

Fuller, C. "King Says Lives Are a Tragedy." *Atlanta Journal*, 1 July 1974, 2.

Garrett, F. M. *Yesterday's Atlanta*. Miami: E.A. Seemann Publishing, Inc., 1974.

————. "An Atlanta Quiz." *Atlanta Constitution Sunday Magazine and Feature Section*, 9 June 1940, 4.

————. *Atlanta and Environs I*. Athens, GA: University of Georgia Press, 1987.

————. *Atlanta and Environs II*. Athens, GA: University of Georgia Press, 1987.

Garrison, W. *The Legacy of Atlanta, A Short History*. Atlanta, Georgia: Peachtree Publishers, 1987.

Goss, S. *Atlanta: Peach of a City* (audio cassette), Volume I. Atlanta: Jacor Broadcasting, WPCH-FM,
    1987.

————. *Atlanta: Peach of a City* (audio cassette), Volume II. Atlanta: Jacor Broadcasting, WPCH-FM,
    1987.

Green, C. "Naming Park for Klansman, Stone Mountain Rescinds." *Atlanta Journal*, 3 August 1988.

Gwin, Y. *Yolande's Atlanta*. Atlanta: Peachtree Publishers, 1983.

Haines, M. Personal interview.

Ham, T. "Death, Horror, and Destruction Could Smite Atlanta Any Day." *Atlanta Journal*, 19 February 1942, 8.

Harwell, R., ed. *"Gone With the Wind" as Book and Film.* Columbia University of South Carolina Press, 1983.

Hays, S., and Goodwin, A. *The Winecoff Fire.* Atlanta: Longstreet Press, 1993.

Hayslet, C. "FBI Sought Disbarment of KKK Chief." *Atlanta Journal*, 25 November 1977, 10A.

Hendrick, B. "The Riches under Rich's." *Atlanta Journal-Constitution*, 10 July 1994, 1B.

Hepburn, L.R. *The Georgia History Book.* Athens: Institute of Government University of Georgia, 1982.

Herndon Family Biographies. Atlanta: The Herndon House.

"Heroic Mother Saves Child; Another Drops 2, Then Leaps." *Atlanta Journal*, 8 December 1946, 8A.

History of Pike County, 1822–1989. Dallas: Curtis Media Corporation, 1989.

Hoehling, A. *Last Train from Atlanta.* Harrisburg, Pennsylvania: Stackpole Books, 1992.

Hoffman, P. "Creating Underground Atlanta, 1898–1932." *Atlanta Historical Bulletin*, September 1968, 13: 55–65.

Hopkins, S. "Secret's Out: Donor is Woodruff." *Atlanta Constitution*, 12 July 1974, 1, 18A.

Hornady, J. R. *Atlanta Yesterday, Today, and Tomorrow.* American Cities Book Company, 1922.

Hudspeth, R. "Beware If You See This Girl on Halloween," *Atlanta Journal*, 31 October 1981, 1B.

Hunter, S. *75 Years Between the Peachtrees, a History of Crawford W. Long Memorial Hospital of Emory University.* Atlanta: Susan Hunter Publishing, 1987.

"Indictment Sought after Baseball Gambling Raid." *Atlanta Constitution*, 22 August 1946, 1.

"Ivan the Gorilla." News report. Seattle: KING-TV, 10 October 1994.

Jenkins, H. "My Most Bizarre Murder Case." *Atlanta Journal and Constitution Magazine,* 22 August 1971, 12.

Jones, C. F. *Mistakes That Worked.* New York: Doubleday Book for Young Readers, 1991.

King, A. W. "Atlanta's First Ballpark." *Atlanta Historical Bulletin*, December 1947, VIII: 12–16.

———. "Evolution of the Wheel or Perils of Early Bicycling in Atlanta." *Atlanta Historical Bulletin*, December, 1947, VIII(32): 1–8.

King, C. S. *My Life with Martin Luther King, Jr.*, New York: Avalon Books, 1970.

Kurtz, A. L. F. "Departed Glory of State Square." *Atlanta Journal Magazine,* 1 December 1935, 2+.

Laccetti, S. "130th Anniversary The Battle of Atlanta." *Atlanta Journal-Constitution*, 17 July 1994, 1D+.

Lawing, P. Personal interview, 17 September 1994.

Lawson, S. "Minorities Find a Friend in National Klan Wizard." *Macon Telegraph*, 27 July 1978, 1A.

Light, J. Personal interview, 27 June 1994.

"London Calls All Day on Hotel Fire." *Atlanta Journal*, 8 December 1946, 14A.

Mankin, W. Personal interview, 14 September 1994.

Martin, H. *Atlanta and Environs III.* Athens, GA: University of Georgia Press, 1987.

Matthews, A. J. *Oakdale Road, Atlanta, Georgia, Dekalb County: Its History and Its People.* Atlanta: self-published, 1972.

Mason, J. W. "Atlanta's Matronymic," Speeches and Articles, Unpublished Manuscript #158/DU–28–15, Box 1, File 2, Atlanta History Center.

McCallie, S.W. "An Atlanta Quiz." *Atlanta Constitution Sunday Magazine and Feature Section*, 26 May 1940, 4.

McCullar, B. *This Is Your Georgia.* Montgomery, AL: Viewpoint Publications, 1972.

McKee, R. "Guests Saved in Downtown Hotel Blaze." *Atlanta Journal*, 19 February 1942, 1, 16.

Merritt, C. Personal interview, 17 June 1994.

Mitchell, E. M. "Marthasville and Atlanta." Speeches and Articles, Unpublished Manuscript #158/ DU–28–15, Box 1, File 2. Atlanta History Center.

———. "Queer Place Names in Old Atlanta." *Atlanta Historical Bulletin,* April 1931, 5: 21–22.

———. *A Brief History of Atlanta Public School System* by W. W. Gaines, 1922. Manuscript collection. MSS 158. Atlanta History Center.

———. Letter to J. L. Edgerton, Western Newspaper Union. Manuscript #158/DU–28–14, Box 1, File 1, 1894–1928. Atlanta History Center.

Moore, J. H. "Atlanta's Hanson Car." *Atlanta Historical Bulletin,* June 1967, 12: 16–28.

Morris, M. "Rich's to Rage." *Atlanta Journal-Constitution*, 4 June 1994, 2B.

Neal, W. "A Big City Hospital's 75 Years." *Atlanta Journal and Constitution Magazine*, 26 February 1967, 8.

Neiss, E. Personal interview, 19 August 1994.

Oney, S. "The Search for Jim Conley." *Atlanta Journal-Constitution*, 12 August 1990, 1M.

Park, H. "Hundreds Visit Grady's Morgue in Effort to Identify Victims." *Atlanta Journal*, 8 December 1946, 14A.

Patton, D. A. Personal interview, Zebulon, Georgia, 26 May 1994.

"People Quick to Answer Blood Call." *Atlanta Journal*, 8 December 1946, 6A.

"Photo Showed Guardian Angel at Margaret Mitchell's Doorway." *Atlanta Constitution*, 16 June 1960.

"Police Raid Ponce de Leon Bleachers." *Atlanta Constitution*, 22 August 1946, 1.

Posnanski, J. "Aaron's Escorts." *Georgia Alumni Record*, September 1994, 73: 21–23.

Radford, R. L. *Prelude to Fame, Crawford Long's Discovery of Anaesthesia* [sic]. Los Altos, CA: Geron-X, Inc., 1969.

Reeves, N. Personal interview, Zebulon, Georgia, 1 November 1994.

"Remember Them Monday Nights When the Siren Sounds." *Atlanta Journal*, 23 August 1942, 2A.

Shaara, M. *The Killer Angels*. New York: Balantine Books, 1974.

Schonbak, J. "Five Years Later It's Still 'Superport.'" *Business Atlanta*, March 1985, 148–150.

———. "Rich Man, Poor Man, Carpetbagger—Thief?" *Business Atlanta,* November 1982, 79–81.

———. "Rose Mansion Built from 'Medicine Whiskies' Profits." *Business Atlanta,* November 1986, 112–113.

———. "Up from the Ashes: The 1917 Fire." *Business Atlanta*, November 1985, 126–128.

———. "The Hawking Hucksters of Humbug Square." *Business Atlanta*, April 1985, 130–132.

Seabrook, C. "Atlanta's Zoo Ranked in Bottom 10." *Atlanta Constitution*, 15 February 1984, 1.

Shannon, M. "Fire Makes Grady Hospital Giant Morgue, House of Grief." *Atlanta Journal*, 8 December 1946, 13A.

Shavin, N. *Days in the Life of Atlanta*. Atlanta: Capricorn Corporation, 1987.

Shavin, N., and Galphin, B. *Atlanta: Triumph of a People*. Atlanta: Capricorn Corporation, 1985.

Sibley, C. *Dear Store, An Affectionate Portrait of Rich's*. Atlanta, Georgia: Peachtree Publishers, 1967.

———. "Two Governors (series)." *Atlanta Constitution*, 30 June 1974, 12; 1 July 1974, 3B; 2 July 1974, 5B; 3 July 1974, 3B.

Steedman, M. "Ghost in a Fruit Jar." *Atlanta Journal Magazine*, 20 June 1967, 11.

Suit, H. Personal interview, Atlanta, Georgia, 3 October 1994.

"Surprise 5-County Black-Out Planned." *Atlanta Journal*, 23 August 1942, 2A.

Talmadge, B. Personal interview, Lovejoy, Georgia, 16 August 1994.

Tate, J. H. "Keeper of the Flame." *The Story of Atlanta Gas Light Company*. Atlanta, Georgia: Atlanta Gas Light Company, 1985.

Taylor, M.R. Personal interview, 17 September 1994.

Taylor, R. "Odd Adventures Are Hallmark of Zoo." *Atlanta Constitution*, 10 June 1984, 18A.

———. "Prairie Dog Holes Filled With Concrete." *Atlanta Constitution*, 3 June 1984.

———. "'Twinkles' Last Day a Mystery." *Atlanta Constitution*, 25 May 1984.

Thornton, E. M. "An Atlanta Quiz." *Atlanta Constitution Sunday Magazine and Feature Section*, 16 June 1940, 4.

Tibbits, G. "Urban Gorilla." Associated Press, 11 October 1994.

Troop, P., and Walker, T. "Krofft World Park Closed by Owners." *Atlanta Journal*, 12 March 1976, 24A.

Underwood, D. Personal interview, 15 March 1994.

Walker, M. *Margaret Mitchell & John Marsh, The Love Story behind Gone With the Wind*. Atlanta: Peachtree Publishers, 1993.

Watson-Powers, L. " Atlanta Spirit, What Is It?" *Atlanta Historical Society Bulletin*, Fall 1993, 83–84.

Welcome South Brother. Atlanta, Georgia: WSB Radio, 1974.

Wells, T.L. "Easy Cradle Ripoff." *Atlanta Constitution*, 8 January 1979, 2C.